BRAD

BRAD

The unofficial and unauthorised biography of
BRAD PITT
by Adam Phillips

Published by
Kandour Ltd
1-3 Colebrook Place
London N1 8HZ

This edition printed in 2004 for
Bookmart Limited
Registered Number 2372865
Trading as Bookmart Ltd
Blaby Road
Wigston
Leicester LE18 4SE

First published June 2004

ISBN 1–904756–11–5

Production services:
Metro Media Ltd

Author: Adam Phillips

With thanks to: Jenny Ross, Emma Hayley,
Lee Coventry & Paula Field

Cover design: Mike Lomax
Cover Image: Rex Features

Inside images: Rex Features

© Kandour Ltd

Printed and bound by Nørhaven Paperback, Denmark

BRAD PITT

FOREWORD

This series of biographies is a celebration of celebrity. It features some of the world's greatest modern-day icons including movie stars, soap personalities, pop idols, comedians and sporting heroes. Each biography examines their struggles, their family background, their rise to stardom and in some cases their struggle to stay there. The books aim to shed some light on what makes a star. Why do some people succeed when others fail?

Written in a light-hearted and lively way, and coupled with the most up-to-date details on the world's favourite heroes and heroines, this series is an entertaining read for anyone interested in the world of celebrity. Discover all about their career highlights – what was the defining moment to propel them into superstardom? No story about fame is without its ups and downs. We reveal the emotional rollercoaster ride that many of these stars have been on to stay at the top. Read all about your most adored personalities in these riveting books.

BRAD PITT

CONTENTS

BRAD PITT

FACT FILE

Full Name: William Bradley Pitt
Eye Colour: Blue
Date of Birth: 16 December 1963
Place Of Birth: Shawnee, Oklahoma, USA
Height: 5' 11"
Marriages: Jennifer Aniston (2000 - present day)
Children: None

Star sign: Sagittarius (Nov 23 – Dec 21)
Archers are known for aiming at a target and hitting the bullseye. Highly creative, they are good natured, passionate and are happy to air their views. In love, they are uncomplicated and sincere, preferring straight talking to complex relationships. They are also imaginative and erotic lovers. Sagittarians are known to wander because they are too willing to break out of the confinements of work and responsibility.

BRAD PITT

Chinese birth sign: Rabbit

Typically strong willed, unobtrusive, systematic, confident, and don't like disagreements. Their live and let live attitude means than they don't usually get into trouble or make enemies. They are also known for their kindness and thoughtfulness to others. The sign is also the symbol of long life.

Career High: In 1996 he played a manic-depressive Jeffrey Goines in Terry Gilliam's *Twelve Monkeys* for which Pitt was nominated for Best Supporting Actor at the Academy Awards. He won Best Performance by an Actor in a Supporting Role in a Motion Picture at the Golden Globes.

1

Pretty boy done pretty darn good

BRAD PITT

PRETTY BOY DONE PRETTY DARN GOOD

Earlier this year, twins Mike and Matt Schlepp appeared on MTV as cameras filmed them blowing thousands of dollars on plastic surgery. And no, they didn't have some lurid growth on their faces that desperately needed corrective surgery. Nope, the two 'aspiring' actors had their eyes (and chin implants) aimed squarely on one goal – to make themselves look more like film star Brad Pitt.

Mike and Matt endured two months of pain recovering from the surgery and while they claim that they are delighted with the results, anyone will have genuine difficulty in seeing any similarities

PRETTY BOY DONE PRETTY DARN GOOD

between the two boys from Arizona and the golden boy of Hollywood, Brad Pitt.

While the press printed the pictures of them before and after and lambasted TV for sinking to new depths, what the story really illustrated was just how far Brad Pitt's appeal has embedded itself in popular culture; that Pitt, the middle class boy from Missouri, has come a long, long way.

What he made of the twins' struggle to become more like him is unknown. And irrelevant. After all, here is the guy who's starred in over 20 movies which combined have drawn over a billion dollars at the box office; who lives in Beverly Hills in a house worth $13.5 million; who has been declared the world's sexiest man alive twice by *People Magazine*; oh, and who also happens to be married to *Friends* phenomena and up-and-coming movie star, Jennifer Aniston – and their marriage has already lasted nearly four years. Which is three lifetimes in Hollywood terms.

Not a bad lot for someone who, in his first few steps up the Hollywood career ladder, was seen by some cynics as no more than a mere pretty boy – eye candy for the ladies at best; a one-trick pony bound for the Tinseltown abattoir at worst.

Indeed, while those twins, Mike and Matt,

BRAD PITT

PRETTY BOY DONE PRETTY DARN GOOD

believe their cosmetic surgery can only help their careers in Tinseltown, Brad Pitt has always known that good looks can help you in the very short term – but can easily end up turning on you and biting you on your pert butt when you're trying to gain credibility as a serious actor.

And while his first career breaks may have come in the shape of playing a chisel-jawed empty head in three episodes of Dallas and appearing as a spunky hunk in a Levi's ad, Brad Pitt has gone on to defy his detractors and spent his career showing that he's more than merely show; he's all go too. From the launch pad that was his scene stealing (and many female fans claim film-stealing) turn in *Thelma And Louise* as the sexual-enlightening bad boy and his character-driven performances in dramas such as *Legends Of The Fall* through to his Oscar-nominated work in *Twelve Monkeys* to his career best as the dark and razor-edged Tyler Durden in *Fight Club*, Pitt has never rested on his laurels. Or his good looks. And the fact that his love life has garnered headlines all over the world hasn't exactly hindered Brad Pitt's profile away from the screen either – linked by the rumour-mongering press to many women, his relationships with the likes of Juliette Lewis were mere

BRAD PITT

sideshows to the main event of Nineties Hollywood gossip which was his doomed coupling with Gwyneth Paltrow. Then of course, in 2000, we had the Hollywood fairytale ending when he tied the silk knot with Jennifer Aniston. Not that it's all been easy-going for the Hollywood hunk – he's experienced defeat at the box office playing death in the dearth-fest that was *Meet Joe Black* and courted controversy with the dud *The Devil's Own*, a cack-handed thriller that Pitt had high hopes for (and had invested a great deal of his time in). But with his easy charm and canny ability to give good interview when confronted by the headline-hungry media, Pitt is quite clearly a Hollywood natural whose meteoric rise from proverbial rags to riches shows no sign of abating.

His impressive track record as a superstar, sex symbol *and* credible actor looks set to continue as Pitt has three films lined up for release over the next year – as Achilles in the Wolfgang Peterson-helmed *Troy*; Rusty Ryan in the sequel *Ocean's Twelve* and the titular Mr Smith in the thriller *Mr & Mrs Smith* alongside Angelina Jolie. In the meantime, Brad Pitt 'look-a-likes', Matt and Mike Schlepp of Arizona are still looking for that big break in Hollywood.

2

Silver spoon
not included

BRAD PITT

SILVER SPOON NOT INCLUDED

Nepotism. It's such an ugly word. It can be very useful though for those people who are born into such an 'ism.' Read biographies or magazine articles on your favourite director, actor (or gaffer) and there's a fair chance that somewhere in their family tree there was invariably someone that helped them get their first break into the movie industry.

While such help can be a double-edged sword, it also makes you respect and admire people who come from less well-connected backgrounds. And you can't get any less well connected than Brad Pitt. He may now command $20,000,000 per movie

SILVER SPOON NOT INCLUDED

but when he was born on 18 December 1963, he wasn't placed into the awaiting arms of a proud Hollywood starlet or movie mogul but a school counsellor Jane Pitt and Bill Pitt, an employee at a trucking company.

Their location? Shawnee, Oklahoma to be precise and shortly after that, Springfield, Missouri – over 1,600 miles away from the Hollywood sign in fact. Two further children, Douglas and Julie, would arrive to complete the Pitt family unit within the next five years but it was Brad who would show signs of being a thespian-in-waiting from an early age.

Brad is happy to acknowledge that it was his mom, Jane, who first realised he had a talent for acting and there were others too who shared her point of view: "You couldn't keep from watching Brad because his face was so expressive," Connie Bilyeu told *People Magazine*. She wasn't a toddler talent scout for Tinseltown but in fact the piano accompanist at the local Baptist Church who realised that even at six-years-old, choirboy Brad had a God's gift for performing.

His love of performance and exhibitionism continued when the young extrovert was enrolled at Kickapoo High School. While he displayed an accomplished academic side, Pitt also busied

SILVER SPOON NOT INCLUDED

himself in student politics, singing, school plays. And of course there was the 'group' The Brief Boys which involved Pitt and his chums blasting out Beach Boys songs with their own self-penned lyrics; all while dancing round in their underpants to audiences of stunned peers.

But perhaps unsurprisingly, it was his popularity with the opposite sex that some of his fellow students would best remember him for — he'd already garnered himself 'Best Dressed Student' in the Kickapoo yearbook and as a teenager, he was known for his romantic flair. In fact, his relationship with sweetheart and fellow student Sara Hart became so intense that many wondered if the two lovebirds would end up one day getting hitched.

But, alas, it was not meant to be as other sweethearts would follow and perhaps most surprising Pitt would later admit that while at high school there was one girl who he had a crush on but she never even realised it. By the time he hit the seventh grade, Pitt had also become well known for the parties that he'd throw in the basement of his family house. Fellow students would turn up, pull up a bean bag and get to know each other better; probably much to the

SILVER SPOON NOT INCLUDED

disapproval of his mum, Jane, a fully signed-up member of the local Baptist church.

It all sounds like an idyllic life for a teenager – a nurturing and solid family, a secure school life plus a very healthy love life but it wasn't enough for the young Pitt. A regular cinema-goer, perhaps it was his acute love of movies and their stories and locales that made Pitt very much aware of the wider world outside of Springfield, Missouri. His first step in exploring this world came in 1982, when driving an old Buick his dad had given him, Pitt headed to the University of Missouri at Columbia to take up journalism.

Or to be more precise, wild partying at his new frat house, *Sigma Chi*. While at university, Pitt continued his habit of enflaming the lust of the local female population. His desire to show off his physique culminated in posing for a student calendar 'Men of Mizzou' with torso bared and, subsequently, enjoying his role in a strip show which saw female students paying to see Pitt whip nearly all his clothes off in the name of charity.

Like his high school days, Brad Pitt seemed to have the best of all worlds but as he told *US Magazine* in 1991: "Growing up I was like an insider. Inside of everything, like the cool stuff at school – but was always looking out. Because it wasn't quite enough or something."

However, a key event that would shape his future forever soon took place. The first was a collision with a truck that trashed his beloved Buick but thankfully, neither Pitt nor his fellow uni passengers were seriously hurt. The accident made Pitt reevaluate his life and he reasserted his efforts with his studies. Trouble was though that Pitt began realising that the course simply wasn't enough for him.

He was pursuing an advertising strand on his journalism degree but his tutors weren't happy with his left-of-the-middle ad ideas. Pitt became so frustrated that two papers short of attaining his degree and a mere two weeks before graduating, he simply got in his recently acquired Datsun, 'Runaround Sue', and left.

Pitt would later explain that leaving university so near to graduation was obviously not a thought that many students would dare even contemplate so close to 'G-Day'. But when it was almost time to graduate, Pitt suddenly realised how easy leaving would actually be – that all it would entail was packing up his car, pointing it west and flooring the gas pedal.

BRAD PITT

SILVER SPOON NOT INCLUDED

With his decision to escape the small world of Missouri made, Pitt had also decided on his course of action – that he wanted to act; to realise his love of performance and exploit his physical presence while indulging in his self-confessed adoration of the movies. So in 1986, the 22-year-old headed for the city of dreams, LA... and into the awaiting wings of a large, yellow chicken.

3

Tinseltown's the Pitts, man

BRAD PITT

TINSELTOWN'S THE PITTS, MAN

It's perhaps ironic that for all his good looks, toned body and six pack that the first acting gig Brad Pitt landed on his arrival in Hollywood in 1986 was being stuffed inside a huge, yellow-feathered chicken costume. The script for his performance? Clucking at potential clientele about the culinary delights of his employers. His directors? The management of *El Pollo Loco*, fast food restaurant. The location? The corner of Sunset Strip and La Brea Boulevard.

Okay, so it wasn't the most auspicious of starts but it surely must have been better than the previous odd jobs he'd landed when he first drove into Los Angeles. While he has described the drive to the city of dreams itself "as the most exciting time of my life," the real-world practicalities of being a wannabe actor had already dawned on Pitt on his arrival in LA. He subsequently endured the back-busting job of delivering refrigerators to students and hawking products to complete strangers via telemarketing.

And Pitt needed the money – he had arrived in the city of dreams with only $325 in his wallet and needed to cover those irritating costs of living; namely rent and food. Any considerations about asking his folks for a loan was made all the more difficult because Pitt hadn't exactly explained to them that he'd left university early and had decided to become an actor. The fact that he hadn't actually got his degree was something his folks would only find out about later after reading a magazine interview. Before leaving Springfield, he'd simply told them that he was continuing his education by studying at the Art College Center of Design in Pasadena.

Indeed, instead of a cosy campus room, Pitt actually spent the first year and half of his time in the city of dreams sleeping on a floor, sharing a single unfurnished room in Burbank with seven other guys – not that Pitt objected; he just saw his somewhat impoverished accommodation as part of his quest to make it big in Hollywood.

But what the heck, playing that big, yellow chicken was a kind of performance art and one that perhaps inspired Pitt to get dressed up as an ape in an episode of the hellraising, body-mashing TV show *Jackass* 15 years later. And anyway, he could always console himself with his next job – driving strippers to bachelor parties.

Pitt later spoke about this particular job with understandable affection. After all, each night he would drive the girls to the venue – sometimes three shows a night – where they were performing and escort them to their room. As the MC and DJ, he introduced the girls and played the music they wanted, which was usually Prince. As the strippers performed their act, they threw their discarded clothes towards Pitt for safekeeping. He would then ensure that all the girls got paid and with their coffers suitably filled, he'd drive them home.

This driving gig though would also help him get his first leg up the Hollywood ladder and it was one of those girls who pushed him in the direction of the man who had helped Michelle Pfeiffer hone her acting skills in her early days – veteran acting

TINSELTOWN'S THE PITTS, MAN

coach Roy London and Pitt would find himself in a class of 12 budding actors all wanting to have their name up there on Hollywood billboards.

While the acting training was of course vital, perhaps London's greatest gift to Pitt was steeping him in the ways of how the Hollywood movie machine worked when it came to snaring the attentions of casting directors and agents. What he learnt from London began to pay off as he began to turn up to more and more auditions even though Pitt was first to admit that he screwed some of them up "royally". But even London probably wasn't expecting what happened next.

As any actor/actress/waiter in Hollywood will tell you, it's all very well having the physique of Hercules and the acting skills of Tony Blair but without an agent, you may as well stand outside *El Pollo Loco* for the rest of your life. Fortunately for Pitt, one of London's other students needed Pitt's help.

As Pitt explained to *Rolling Stone* magazine: "I was in an acting class. A girl in the class needed a scene partner for an audition for an agent. So I was the scene partner for the audition, and I ended up getting signed." It was a crucial break for Pitt even if his feature film debut in the

TINSELTOWN'S THE PITTS, MAN

adaptation of Bret Easton Ellis's novel, *Less Than Zero*, was less than remarkable. He was an extra who stood in a doorway at a party wearing a pink and white striped top and a pair of sunglasses. He was paid $38.

Pitt then landed the role of a waiter in *No Man's Land*, an unremarkable piece of fluff starring Charlie Sheen. While the film work was proving somewhat underwhelming for Pitt, his TV career suddenly started to look very promising. He was signed up to play Randy, the boyfriend of Priscilla Presley's on-screen daughter in the Eighties' soap phenomena and shoulder pad hell that was *Dallas*.

While he was only in it for a few episodes, the show and his other acting work meant that he could hang up his chicken suit for good and also place a call to his folks to reveal what he'd really been doing in California all this time. Pitt's dad was not surprised to hear the news.

His TV success continued as Pitt notched up a week's work on soap *Another World* and a brief spell in the sitcom, *Growing Pains*. He also enjoyed sharing an episode of *21 Jump Street* with future superstar Johnny Depp.

Pitt's first real brush with celebrity came

TINSELTOWN'S THE PITTS, MAN

with his appearance in *sitcom Head Of The Class* in 1988. But it wasn't because of his acting skills or perfect comedy timing; it was more like celebrity-by-proxy actually – the chins of the Hollywood gossip community were set firmly a-wagging by his rumoured relationship with co-star Robin Givens. She was a hot story at the time as the beleaguered wife of boxing champion Mike Tyson. They had recently split up and for six months, Brad and Givens became very close.

The fact that Mike Tyson was Givens's ex produced some amusing rumours at the time; one of which Pitt commented on in an interview in 1992: "My favourite is that I've been called 'the most frightened man in America.'" A label supposedly born out of an incident that while Pitt was round at Givens' house, Tyson turned up and the golden boy beat a very hasty retreat.

Meanwhile, his acting career was continuing at a steady pace. Pitt had also landed a role in the self-obsessed and angst ridden hit series *Thirtysomething*. While the part wasn't exactly dialogue-heavy, it played an important role in impressing one of the series creators, Edward Zwick, who would end up casting Pitt in *Legends Of The Fall* seven years later.

BRAD PITT

TINSELTOWN'S THE PITTS, MAN

While Pitt may have impressed all and sundry on the set of *Thirtysomething*, he'd also been busy trying to make the leap from starring in sitcoms to acting in movies. By 1988, he'd already appeared as a troublemaker in a made-for-TV movie, *A Stoning In Fulham County*, a story about an Amish family struggling to deal with the horrors of harassment inflicted upon them by their local community.

Pitt's first headlining TV role at that time came in the shape *of Tales From the Crypt*, the hugely popular cult series that can be best described as the demon spawn of *The Twilight Zone* and *Tales Of The Unexpected*. In the episode 'King Of The Road', he played a drag racer who forces a local cop with a secret past into one final race.

Pitt had also been enjoying success in Europe. But it wasn't his acting that was getting him noticed – it was those fine looks and strapping body. His appearance in a 30-second Levi's commercial brought him instant fame in Europe as viewers gazed in adoration as Pitt, playing a prisoner, used his trusty 501s to make a jail break.

In the meantime, Pitt had also auditioned for the role of J.D. in the Michael Lehmann-helmed cult classic *Heathers*. While the casting directors

TINSELTOWN'S THE PITTS, MAN

were impressed with Pitt, they felt that he was "too sweet" for the role and the part of J.D. would eventually end up being given to Christian Slater in a role that would launch the young Jack Nicholson wannabe into stardom.

Pitt probably wasn't too disheartened because firstly, he would end up playing a character called J.D. in the much more popular film *Thelma And Louise* three years later and secondly, the following year, he got his first proper cinematic debut in horror spoof, *Cutting Class* in 1989. True to his emerging typecast, Pitt played a convertible-driving, basketball champ Dwight who delivers such classic lines as: "You know, your father's a lot bigger than I am. Of course, I'm bigger where it really counts!" Needless to say, Pitt ends up saving the day after someone starts killing off the teachers. It's a film that Pitt would confess years later that he's never actually sat down and watched.

1989 was actually a bumper year for Pitt's movie performances – he also appeared in *Happy Together* alongside Helen 'Supergirl' Slater and Patrick Dempsey. The story revolves round students Slater and Dempsey who end up sharing a room together at college after a 'hilarious' mix-up by the housing department. Much mirth

TINSELTOWN'S THE PITTS, MAN

ensues as audiences at the time had to endure the usual cat and dog-like fighting between the couple before they end up falling in love. Caught up in this hilarity was Pitt who played Slater's initial boyfriend.

Then came what seemed to be the perfect opportunity for Pitt – he went and landed his very own TV series in 1990. His audition had impressed the folk at the Fox TV Network who were celebrating after their first year on air. To build on the channel's launch, the network had a raft of new productions ready to snare US audiences and one of their kingpins was a comedy drama *Glory Days* that followed four friends in their post-high school days. Pitt landed the plum role of a former athlete turned reporter, Walker Lovejoy, something of a no-brainer for someone with Pitt's background.

The series hit screens across America, played for six episodes and was promptly zipped up in a body bag and sent to the morgue. As is so often the case with American TV, if a show doesn't start delivering audiences almost immediately, executives start getting night sweats because of their advertisers and pull the plug on a new series before it's had time to build up a dedicated fan base.

BRAD PITT

TINSELTOWN'S THE PITTS, MAN

Undeterred, Pitt was soon back on set. He'd already had a small role as a cameraman in the TV movie *The Image* playing alongside Albert Finney. Then in 1991, he appeared in the film *Across The Tracks* which saw Pitt reprise the usual good looking athletic type.

His most significant role around that time though was in the TV movie *Too Young To Die?* It was important to Pitt for two reasons – the first being that instead of playing the clean-shaven, healthy living ball player-type, Pitt was acting as a street bum who prefers jacking up to jock straps. With a shaggy beard and greasy, unkempt hair, Pitt sized up well as Billy, the character that drags a young, abused girl into a life of drugs, kidnap and murder.

While Pitt delivered his best performance yet, what really caught the attention of the media was his relationship with the young woman playing the lead role in the film – Juliette Lewis. A rising star in her own right, the two fell for each other hard. While Pitt initially had concerns over the age difference – she was 16 compared to his 26 – they moved in with each other soon after filming had finished.

They became the talk of the town. leading

BRAD PITT

TINSELTOWN'S THE PITTS, MAN

Pitt to quip to one interviewer: *"The National Enquirer* has been going through our trash." But unknown to everyone at the time, there was another woman in the offing that would help propel Pitt towards the Hollywood stratosphere. Her name? Thelma...

4

Thelma and Louise...
and Brad

BRAD PITT

A nd to think that Ridley Scott didn't think that Brad Pitt was sexy enough. Back in 1990, Scott was auditioning young actors for the small but perfectly formed role of J.D. in his film *Thelma And Louise*. He needed a young handsome buck to sweep Geena Davis's character Thelma off her feet, help her have her first orgasm, and then steal $6,700 from her before heading off into the night.

William Baldwin had already landed the part but pulled out to go join Kurt Russell in Ron Howard's fire-fighting drama *Backdraft*, and George Clooney had also auditioned for the role but to no avail. At the eleventh hour, Brad Pitt would finally

THELMA AND LOUISE... AND BRAD

step into J.D.'s tight jeans and cowboy hat in a role that would launch his career a proper.

According to *The Calgary Times* movie critic Louis B. Hobson, it was Geena Davis who convinced Scott that Pitt was the right – and sexiest – man for the job. When Hobson was interviewing Davis about her role in kid flick *Stuart Little*, he mentioned Brad Pitt's role as J.D. and her involvement in landing the young up-and-coming star that vital gig: "I knew from the second he walked into the room he was going to be a huge star," recalled Davis.

Hobson goes onto recount that Davis had stepped into a meeting where Scott and his male producers were discussing the potential candidates they'd seen for the part of J.D., and Davis had asked them: "Doesn't anyone want my opinion? Doesn't anyone want a woman's opinion? Take the blond one."

And the rest is history. It's a role that became a talking point round water coolers for women the world over which is impressive for such a small role. After all, J.D. is only on-screen for 14 minutes as Thelma and Louise pick him up while he's hitchhiking and then back in a motel room, J.D. helps Thelma finally understand what she has been missing in the bedroom after years of being married to an abusive, insensitive hubby.

THELMA AND LOUISE... AND BRAD

It's a moment that Pitt jokingly refers to as 'the $6,000 orgasm' because of the cash his character steals from Thelma. And judging from the reaction of female audiences, that sexual enlightening encounter was worth every cent. But shooting the scene wasn't as 'sexy' as one might have thought: "Let me tell you, it was really romantic for all 30 of us in the room," he deadpanned to US Magazine in 1991. "It's a long day when you're running around with a patch over your personals. We were all fighting over what music [to play] to break the tension."

Pitt though would later confess that there was much potential for embarrassment when shooting such steamy scenes alongside Geena Davis: "In one [unused] scene, Geena's sitting in my lap and we're basically naked," he recalled. "You ask yourself what happens if your soldier starts to salute – and at that very moment I ran into that predicament."

Salute or no salute, the film was a hit and garnered controversy in the media – some embracing it as some kind of feminist declaration while others believed that it was in fact anti-feminist. Yet others perhaps more reasonably saw it as a true road movie that simply dealt with those

THELMA AND LOUISE... AND BRAD

classic issues of attaining true freedom.

All of this was irrelevant however for Pitt because here was a part that finally put him on the map and lifted him above all the other pretty boys veering for space on Hollywood billboards. His popularity spilled over into mainstream press as teen mags wrote hormonally-charged articles about the blond, blue-eyed boy. And, of course, Hollywood in its typical fashion of herding itself round like lost sheep in need of a shepherd, started throwing J.D.-like roles at Pitt left, right and centre. But Pitt was having none of it – he wanted to establish himself as a credible actor after all. Unfortunately, his next three flicks would not fare financially as well as *Thelma And Louise*.

First up was the movie *The Favor* that centred round two couples – Pitt and Elizabeth McGovern in one relationship and Harley Jane Kozak and Bill Pullman in the other. The specifics aren't necessary – other than to say Pitt's partner, McGovern, is asked by her friend, Kozak, to sleep with one of Kozak's old flames to see how good he is in the sack.

It's the kind of fluff that even *Coronation Street* script editors might baulk at but perhaps thankfully for Pitt, the film never hit the silver screen because it was shelved due to the financial

THELMA AND LOUISE... AND BRAD

problems that Orion, the film producers, were experiencing. Pitt completists will be delighted to hear though that the film was finally booted onto US videostore shelves in 1994.

Pitt's attraction to playing something different was perfectly illustrated by his first ever lead role in *Johnny Suede*. The film was based on first-time-director Tom DiCillo's one man show *Johnny Suede: Lessons In Love*. While DiCillo did entertain the idea of playing the lead role himself, he eventually decided that using a relative unknown with precious little Hollywood 'persona' was the best way to progress.

After auditioning young actors in New York and then LA, DiCillo was becoming increasingly exasperated at their seeming inability to show they had even the vaguest of grips on Johnny Suede's character. While *Thelma And Louise* had yet to hit the screens, DiCillo was immediately struck by Brad Pitt's audition, which he felt nailed Johnny's underlining character right down to the bone – that for all his bravado, underneath it all Suede was scared witless.

Presumably somewhat relieved, the director gave Pitt the opportunity to fill the suede shoes of the oddball main character; the role was a world

THELMA AND LOUISE... AND BRAD

away from the smouldering J.D. The character of the romantic Johnny Suede boasted the kind of self-belief that was only matched by his own towering ineptitude all topped off with a colossal pompadour, a pair of suede shoes that fall from the sky and an obsessive love of the Fifties.

Johnny Suede was released shortly after *Thelma And Louise* – a fine set of coattails to sweep in on – and, to be frank, if there was ever a film that begged to labelled 'cult classic', this was most definitely it. While the movie wasn't a hit in financial terms, Pitt did receive glowing reviews on both sides of the Atlantic for his performance and the movie, coupled with *Thelma And Louise*, helped solidify his position as being an actor worth keeping a firm eye on in the future.

Then came a major stumble in 1992. It must have seemed like the perfect opportunity for Pitt to slip into something decidedly more commercial. *Cool World* was meant to be a mixture of live action and animation that would leap on the bandwagon of the hugely successful *Who Framed Roger Rabbit?* that had been released four years earlier – indeed, Pitt described the movie as "Roger Rabbit on acid".

Directed by Ralph Bakshi, a veteran of controversial animation, the film tells the story of

THELMA AND LOUISE... AND BRAD

jailbird and cartoonist Jack Deebs (played by Gabriel Byrne) who gets sucked into one of his comic book creations, *Cool World.* In this cartoon world animated character Holli Would (played by Kim Basinger) is desperate to cross over into the real world. The problem? Well, to become real-life flesh and bone, the cartoon character has to sleep with a human.

Cue Pitt as Detective Frank Harris: "Cartoons and humans cannot have sex because it would throw off the balance of the world. So my job is to stop them," explained Pitt at the time. "I know this sounds crazy. Sounded crazy to me, too." And the shoot sounded 'crazy' as well. It was a struggle for all the actors involved because it required so much blue screen work – Pitt confirmed this later by explaining how difficult it is to be natural and impulsive when his co-star was a blue screen.

When the film did finally get released, it received a mauling at the hands of critics and nose dived at the box office. This was proving to be a difficult time for Pitt – after all, he'd not scored – or even been part of – a bona fide box office success in awhile and the one thing about rising stars in Hollywood is that they have a tendency to come crashing back down to earth.

What Pitt really needed was a hit.

BRAD PITT

THELMA AND LOUISE... AND BRAD

Brad's best bits no.1

Thelma And Louise (1991)

Director: Ridley Scott Writer: Calli Khouri
Co-stars: Susan Sarandon, Geena Davis
and Harvey Keitel.

Pitt's role: J.D., the thieving but sexually gratifying drifter.

Plot: two women Thelma and Louise, disillusioned with their lives, take off for the weekend only for Louise to gun down a would-be rapist. The women decide to make a break for Mexico. The only problem? The police are moving in on them. Fast.

Choice character quote: "Well, I've always believed that if done properly, armed robbery doesn't have to be an unpleasant experience." – J.D.

Awards: Best Original Screenplay at the Oscars in 1992 and Best Screenplay – Motion Picture at the Golden Globes in the same year.

THELMA AND LOUISE... AND BRAD

Box office: The film grossed over $45 million in the US alone. Not bad for a film that cost $16.5 million to make. Pitt was paid a rather miserly sum of $6,000 for his role.

Brad's best bits no. 2

Johnny Suede (1992)

Director & writer: Tom DiCillo
Co-Stars: Catherine Keeler, Alison Moir and
Nick Cave.

Pitt's role: The titular Johnny Suede.

Plot: a romantic slice of hyper-reality that follows the adventures of Pitt's character as he tries to become a bona fide musician. And find the woman of his dreams.

Awards: he was nominated for the Grand Jury Prize at the Sundance Film Festival in 1992.

Box office: made for $500,000, the film only racked $55,000 in the US.

5

Beyond good and evil

BEYOND GOOD AND EVIL

Narcissistic is how some critics would choose to describe Robert Redford's decision to cast Brad Pitt in *A River Runs Through It*. Perhaps there was a slither of truth in the accusation as the role of Paul, one of two sons featured in the film, would have been an ideal role for Redford at Pitt's age. Couple this with the fact that many pundits had been gushing about Pitt looking like a young Robert Redford, and any jaded critic's cynicism was bound to go into overdrive. But even Pitt didn't want to be labelled: "Everyone wants to say you're James Dean and later they want to say you're gay," he said in 1995.

BRAD PITT

BEYOND GOOD AND EVIL

"People just amaze me that they want to get you classified."

For the rest of us cinema-going folk though, putting Brad Pitt in the movie made absolute sense – after all, here was the ideal person to play a golden boy who descends into self-destruction.

While Pitt confesses that he was very unhappy with his first audition for Robert Redford and had even sent in a second audition on videotape, Redford himself had already been keeping an eye on Pitt's burgeoning career and was convinced that Pitt was the ideal actor to play Paul: "[He] had an inner conflict that was very interesting to me," Redford would later comment.

The film, based on the autobiographical book by the now deceased writer Norman Maclean, portrays the relationship between a father (played by Tom Skerrit) and his two sons, Norman and Paul (played by Craig Sheffer and Pitt respectively). The one thing that binds them all together is their love of fly-fishing – a skill that Pitt went to great pains to master when he was preparing himself for the role. Before heading out to the filming locations in Montana, Pitt practised at a friend's swimming pool, managing to catch his own head on more than one occasion. More important to Pitt than his attempt at fly-fishing was working with Redford who became something of a mentor figure for the young performer.

A River Runs Through It was released in 1992 to warm reviews and respectable box office returns. Pitt's performance though seemed to divide opinion – while some would say that his performance was superficial and callow, others would rave that his portrayal of Paul contained genuine depth. Pitt himself was quite frank about any issues he had with the character of Paul: "Of my part, there could've been more underneath, in my opinion," Pitt told *Movieline Magazine* in 1993. "Little more back-story, maybe. But there's no getting around it. Redford did a fantastic job crafting that film, shaping it into chiselled granite."

The film was enough to pull Pitt back from the edge after his two previous films had fared poorly at the box office. More importantly, if *A River Runs Through It* was the zenith of Brad Pitt capitalising on his good looks then his next role would show that if there's one thing that separates Pitt from his peers, it's perhaps the size of his cojones. Well, proverbially speaking at least.

While Pitt could have sauntered off, riding on the hype of his golden boy image and indulging

BEYOND GOOD AND EVIL

himself (and his fans) in continuously being labelled as the new James Dean or Robert Redford, he didn't. Instead he decided to play the grotesque character Early Grayce in the stylish but flawed *Kalifornia*.

Shot by music director Dominic Sena, it tells the story of two pretentious city yuppies, Brian Kessler and Carrie Laughlin (played by David Duchovny and Michelle Forbes). Presumably to escape their middle-class malaise, they decide to hit the roads of the US to research a book on serial killers with Kessler writing the prose while Laughlin snaps pictures of infamous locations that are connected to the murderers.

In a convoluted but gloriously Hollywood twist of fate, they end up riding shotgun with Early Grayce and his trailer trash girlfriend Adele Corners. Grayce, though, happens to be no stranger to all things killer and serial – he's a full-blown psycho with a short fuse and a string of corpses to his name.

As Pitt would tell reporters at the time, his character was a redneck; a hillbilly from the backwoods with no sense of morality, who kills people as others would kill an insect. Grayce hasn't had many opportunities in life and fewer choices so he has made his own decisions on what

BEYOND GOOD AND EVIL

is right and wrong. He makes things up to stop himself from getting bored and one of his 'pastimes' is murder.

While TV audiences had already seen Pitt playing a bad boy from the wrong side of the tracks in *Too Young To Die?* back in 1990, Kalifornia's Grayce was a walkin', talkin' body bag of hate. Pitt trashed his golden boy image by sporting a scraggy beard plus tattoos, scars and even a chipped tooth; a breakage brought about by Pitt accidentally chipping his tooth while using his mouth as an improvised bottle opener.

While he did put on weight for the role of Grayce, Pitt was quick to point out that he's no method actor. Pitt admitted to doing very little research for his roles. Although he is aware that many actors immerse themselves into their characters for months at a time, Pitt explained that for character research on *Kalifornia,* he simply started to read a book about a serial killer and after the first 20 or so pages, he felt he'd got the drift of drifter Grayce.

Kalifornia also threw up another unique opportunity for Pitt – to have his off-screen girlfriend Juliette Lewis play Grayce's on-screen belle. It was another ideal casting for the producers

BEYOND GOOD AND EVIL

as well because Lewis's own career was already beginning to kick off big time after her performances in Woody *Allen's Husbands And Wives* and in Martin Scorsese's remake of *Cape Fear* alongside Robert De Niro.

Lewis and Pitt's coupling in a movie made sense off-screen as well – the lovebirds had been separated over long periods of time because of their individual filming commitments and it was beginning to play on the relationship.

Like the film's subject matter, shooting *Kalifornia* in Atlanta was gruelling. The cast and crew had to endure torrential rain, soaring temperatures plus an earthquake and its aftershocks. Despite all the effort, the film came and went at the box office.

Perhaps audiences didn't want to see Pitt playing a really bad guy. Or perhaps it was because the film had no real likeable character (with the possible exception of Lewis). Or perhaps it was because the film's characters were more featherweight than heavyweight. 'Pretentious' was also a word banded about by critics on the film's release but it wasn't all bad news.

If the film showed one thing, it was that Pitt had no fear of taking his celebrity persona, his

BEYOND GOOD AND EVIL

golden boy looks and his adoring female fans and disposing of them like Grayce would one of his victims. And it was a performance that showed Tinseltown that he could do 'diversity' and a role that won him favour with the critics – "[He's] all boyish charm and then a snort that exudes pure menace," wrote Peter Travers in *Rolling Stone*.

Even his turn in the Quentin Tarantino-penned *True Romance* shortly afterwards in 1993 showed that Pitt enjoyed playing the antithesis of his golden boy persona – even if it was in a comic turn as the scene-stealing doped-up couch potato, Floyd. Anyone alive at the time will remember that Tarantino was Hollywood's latest darling and his back catalogue of scripts written while working in a video store, were flying off his PC's hard drive and on to the big screen.

British director Tony Scott was bringing Tarantino's story of a hell-raising, on-the-run couple, Clarence Worley and Alabama Whitman (played by Christian Slater and Patricia Arquette) to the big screen. He had already attracted heavy weight actors like Christopher Walken and Dennis Hopper who had hopped on board in small roles because they, like everyone else, loved Tarantino's turn of phrase on the page. And so did Brad Pitt

BEYOND GOOD AND EVIL

who contacted Scott to see if there was any room left for him in the movie.

Enter Floyd, a small but perfectly formed cameo who's the flatmate of Worley's best chum in LA. Pitt readily admits that his portrayal of the character was based on a guy who had crashed at his place in LA – the houseguest came for a few days but ended up growing into Pitt's couch after extending his stay for several months.

Pitt's role was a scene-stealer not only for the pure comedy value of seeing the golden boy acting as if he's stoned off his pecks but because the well-meaning character Floyd inadvertently manages to set up the deaths of pretty much everyone in the film. It was a plum and very well received role and more importantly, one perhaps that would offer Pitt a respite before embarking on the most important role of his career to date – starring in *Legends Of The Fall* alongside the legendary Anthony Hopkins.

But before that, there was the issue of his failing relationship with Juliette Lewis to deal with.

6

The golden boy grows up

BRAD PITT

THE GOLDEN BOY GROWS UP

Scientology would prove to be the last nail in the coffin for Brad Pitt and Juliette Lewis's relationship. The organisation created by sci-fi writer L. Ron Hubbard in the Fifties claims to help people get rid of the negative forces that burden them (and their careers) by hooking up to a machine called the E-meter.

For any budding Hollywood actor — to outsiders at least, Scientology is to Tinseltown what the Freemason's is to the UK's police force. In other words, once you're in, the hope surely is that you'll soon be networking with the industry's top people who are also Scientologists, as well as being

THE GOLDEN BOY GROWS UP

spiritually enlightened.

Having successful actors on board such as John Travolta must also act as excellent, walkin' talkin' billboard for anyone hoping to progress up the career and spiritual enlightenment ladder.

Juliette Lewis had been interested in Scientology for over a decade and by the Nineties was becoming more and more involved. Her relationship with Pitt was already precarious because both spent so much time apart shooting their own individual projects and, according to reports at the time, Lewis was also keen to tie the knot – something that Pitt simply wasn't ready for.

While Lewis never forced Scientology on Pitt, he did in fact attend a few of their classes to see what all the fuss was about. But Scientology simply didn't sit well with him.

So their relationship finally wound up, something that Pitt seemed almost blasé about in an interview in 1994: "We had one [a relationship] for about three years, then we didn't have one. We still hang out. I see her a lot, but it's hard with two actors together."

Not even an offer from Oliver Stone for Pitt and Lewis to play those lovable lunatics Mickey and Mallory Knox in *Natural Born Killers*

THE GOLDEN BOY GROWS UP

could've helped save their relationship because Pitt simply wasn't interested in playing another Early Grayce-esque character. And besides, his past was about to catch up with him in the shape of Edward Zwick.

The co-creator of *Thirtysomething,* Zwick had subsequently carved out a successful career as a director of such films as *About Last Night* and *Glory.* He was now looking for people to cast in his latest epic *Legends Of The Fall*, a movie based on the 81-page novella by Jim Harrison.

Zwick hadn't forgotten about Pitt's attention-grabbing turn in *Thirtysomething* and had already approached Pitt even before *Thelma And Louise* had hit the big screen about the part of Tristan, one of three brothers living a cut-off life with their father away from modern life in the Rocky Mountains. The golden boy was interested back then and with the film's production looking a certainty, Pitt came on board, taking a deferred fee.

Then Anthony Hopkins, delighted at the opportunity to star in his first ever 'Western', signed up to play Pitt's father, the anti-establishment Colonel Ludlow, and Henry Thomas, most famous for the blubbing Elliot in *ET*, took on the role of Pitt's younger brother Samuel and Aidan Quinn was brought on board to play the eldest brother, Alfred. The final kingpin to fall into place – or queenpin in this case – was Julia Ormond who was an up-and-coming star back in Britain who would take on the role of Susannah Finncannon whose arrival at the Ludlow home tests the bonds between the three brothers.

Even with such a stellar cast alongside him, *Legends Of The Fall* was a colossal responsibility for Pitt – the entire film would rest on his successful portrayal of his character as shooting started in Calgary. Producer Marshall Herskovitz gave Pitt some key advice on playing the part of Tristan: "Marshall said something to me in the beginning that kind of grooved things for me," said. "What you see on the page is a guy [Tristan] gutting animals, a guy who's scalped people, who breaks horses, all this stuff. But because of all that stuff, you can let him feel all the more, right?' Marshall said, 'You have the luxury here to feel as much as you want.'"

While such words of wisdom may have helped Pitt get a handle on the role, there were signs of mounting pressure. While director Zwick would joke that shooting an epic on the scale of *Legends Of The Fall* must be something akin to the pain of childbirth, Pitt would soon clash with Zwick over

THE GOLDEN BOY GROWS UP

his interpretation of the Tristan character. It was rumoured that there was an angry dispute between actor and director during the shooting of the jail scene where Julia Ormond's character visits Tristan in jail. Because of Pitt's commitment to *Interview With The Vampire* which would start shooting very shortly, it meant that Pitt's scenes all had to be shot early. And he wasn't happy with such an emotionally loaded climatic scene being shot in the first week.

"The jail scene wasn't right, wasn't written right, didn't fit in," he said. An argument, between Zwick and Pitt ensued – reports suggest that the argument was so intense that furniture ended up being thrown across the set. Pitt later justified the argument saying that it was in fact good because when two people care so much about something, the end results will inevitably reflect this. And thankfully, they did.

Although the news of the spat would reach the ears of Hollywood's gossip mongerers and led to an outbreak of negative speculation about the production, Pitt insisted later that the rest of the shoot was "pretty easy-going" from then on in. A matter no doubt helped by the fact that Pitt was convinced that the character of Tristan in *Legends*

THE GOLDEN BOY GROWS UP

Of The Fall was made for him. He would state during the film's shoot that with his other roles, he always felt that there were other actors out there who could have played those parts better. With the character of Tristan, Pitt knew he was the best man for the job – he knew 'the corners and bends' that the hot-headed Tristan's character takes.

But the experience of playing Tristan did have an effect on Pitt – despite his aversion to the idea of method acting where actors 'become' their characters for the duration of a production, Pitt found that he was emotionally drained by the role of the wild-at-heart Tristan.

But there was to be no respite for Pitt as he had to go straight into shooting *Interview With The Vampire* in a role that would prove to be even darker and more punishing than that of Tristan's. He was to play the vampire Louis de Pointe du Lac, a depressed and tortured immortal in a film that was already causing controversy before a single frame had even been shot.

The author Anne Rice had penned the original novel back in 1976 in attempt to come to terms with the death of her five-year-old daughter. While many publishers initially baulked at publishing the book because of its

THE GOLDEN BOY GROWS UP

pitch-black nature, it eventually hit bookstands and became a bestseller.

A movie version starring John Travolta had been touted about and then at one time Richard Chamberlain was to star in a TV mini-series adaptation; there were also reports that Elton John was sniffing round the book and its sequel for the basis of a musical. Eventually though, music mogul David Geffen was offered the opportunity to bring *Interview With The Vampire* to the big screen. And that's when the *real* problems kicked off. Rice *was* very happy to be asked to write the book's big screen adaptation and was equally thrilled with the choice of Irishman Neil Jordan as director who she loved because of his film *Company Of Wolves* back in 1984. But her delight soon turned to horror.

First of all, Jordan went on to extensively rewrite her script – "the story didn't work," he said. "I had to bring the moral dilemma [of Louis's character] to the forefront." He also wanted the trio of Louis, Lestat and the young girl Claudia to operate more as a bizarre family unit brought together by their extreme loneliness. While the rewrites may have stirred up trouble, Jordan then went and announced who he had lined up for the cast. Anne Rice had no problem with Pitt being cast as Louis. Nope, her problem was with Tom Cruise being cast as Louis's turner and ultimately nemesis, Lestat.

And boy, oh, boy did she let her dissatisfaction at Jordan's decision be known on the infamous day of 22 August 1993: "I was particularly stunned by the casting of Cruise…" she spat in an interview with *The Los Angeles Times*. "I am puzzled as to why Cruise would want to take on the role… (He) should do himself a favour and withdraw."

Rice's unhappiness was nothing though compared to her fans who were sending in hate mail and holding demonstrations against the film before a single frame had even been shot. While Cruise took all of her stinging criticism in his stride, Geffen and Jordan would also stand firm by their decision – their faith in Cruise's acting skills was most probably dwarfed by the idea of having two such huge stars headlining in the same movie.

More casting chaos ensued as the production lost the actor who was to play the Malloy, the journalist who questions the Louis character about his ghoulish past. River Phoenix, a young man already well on his way to stardom, collapsed outside The Viper Room, a nightclub owned by

THE GOLDEN BOY GROWS UP

Johnny Depp in LA, and died on the way to the hospital from a drug overdose.

Because of the tragedy, Christian Slater took over Phoenix's role and the production finally got underway. The five and a half month shooting schedule proved punishing for Pitt because the character of Louis was such a depressive and he'd had precious little prep time in between *Legends Of The Fall* and *Interview With The Vampire*.

Life wasn't made any easier by the reports coming from the set that Cruise's voice was supposedly too 'reedy', that he was wearing stacked heeled to make his character taller and that he and Pitt weren't exactly becoming bosom buddies. More importantly to everyone involved on the production though would be Rice's reaction on seeing the finished film. After all, if she started spitting nails again in press interviews, it really wouldn't be doing the film's chances of hitting gold at the box office any favours whatsoever.

A preview tape was duly dispatched to Rice and shortly afterwards, the author spent close to $100,000 taking out adverts in *The New York Times, The Los Angeles Times* and *Variety*. The double page ads stated: "The charm, the humour and the invincible innocence of my beloved hero

THE GOLDEN BOY GROWS UP

Lestat are all alive in Tom Cruise's courageous performance; the guilt and suffering of Louis are poignantly portrayed by Brad Pitt... I think you will embrace this film as I do."

And US audiences certainly did – the film's word-of-mouth probably also helped in part by Oprah Winfrey's confession on her show when interviewing Tom Cruise that she had walked out of a preview screening because the movie was too disturbing for her tastes. The film subsequently cleaned up at the box office, raking in $38.7 million in its first weekend alone before going on to drum up $105 million in the US. In the meantime, while Pitt had shot his scenes for *Legends Of The Fall* before *Interview With The Vampire*, the epic ended up being released a month after the vamp flick. And it went down even better with audiences, staying at number one for four weeks in a row.

More importantly, Pitt took his entire family along to see *Legends Of The Fall* on Christmas Day in 1994 and, thankfully, they loved it.

BRAD PITT

THE GOLDEN BOY GROWS UP

Brad's best bits no. 3

Legends Of The Fall (1994)

Director: Edward Zwick
Writers: Susan Shilliday and William D. Wittliff
Co-Stars: Anthony Hopkins, Aidan Quinn and Julia Ormond

Pitt's role: As the wild man, Tristan Ludlow.

Plot: set in the early 1900s, Colonel Ludlow brings up his three sons in the isolation of Montana to shield them from American society which he has come to loathe. The bonds between the three brothers seems to be unbreakable until Susanna Finncannon arrives to shake the family to its very foundations.

Choice character quote: "Miss Finncannon. It's a pleasure to meet you. I hope you and ugly here find every happiness together," said by Tristan.

Awards: it won a Best Cinematography Oscar and gleaned Pitt a Golden Globe nomination for his performance as Tristan.

BRAD PITT

THE GOLDEN BOY GROWS UP

Box office: For such a stellar cast, its $30 million budget is modest and it went on to claim nearly $70 million at the US box office alone.

Brad's best bits no. 4

Interview With The Vampire (1994)

Director: Neil Jordan
Writer: Anne Rice
Co-Stars: Tom Cruise, Kirsten Dunst and Christian Slater

Pitt's role: As moribund vampire, Louis de Pointe du Lac.

Plot: at the end of the 20th century, Louis recounts his (eternal) life story through the ages to an interviewer. Turned into a vampire by Lestat de Lioncourt, Louis has had it tough as a vampire, loathing the idea of taking human life to feed his own vampiric urges and is haunted by his troubled relationship with Lestat. Trouble is wherever Louis is, Lestat is never far behind.

BRAD PITT

THE GOLDEN BOY GROWS UP

Choice character quote: "Most of all I longed for death. I know that now. I invited it. A release from the pain of living. My invitation was open to anyone. To the whore at my side, to the pimp that followed. But it was a vampire that accepted," said Louis to the interviewer.

Awards: well, Pitt certainly hit pay dirt (of sorts) with his portrayal of Louis – he won both Best Actor and Most Desirable Male at the MTV Movie Awards.

Box office: the $50 million budgeted movie raised an impressive $105 million at the US box office and nearly £10 million in the UK.

7

A seven pack and a Paltrow

BRAD PITT

A SEVEN PACK AND A PALTROW

W hat's in the box? What's in the f****** box!" the young, beaten-up cop looks up at his ageing partner and then back down at the serial killer knelt in front of him. The confusion, bewilderment and mounting horror that flashes across his face in those few seconds reflected exactly how the audience felt as they sat there squirming in the darkness as they looked up at the living hell playing out on the big screen.

What follows is the expectation-shattering denouement to the remarkable thriller *Seven*. While serial killer movies had been flogged, beaten and mutilated to death by a mass of Hollywood

A SEVEN PACK AND A PALTROW

flicks (including Pitt in *Kalifornia* two years before), *Seven* was an original – a standout film that crushed the serial killer bandwagon under foot, and stood out as a classic in its own right.

More importantly, *Seven* was the film that Brad Pitt had finally decided to do next after *Interview With The Vampire* and *Legends Of The Fall*. He was now a bona fide A-list star and Hollywood wanted him in everything – he'd already turned down roles in *City Hall*, *The Saint* and had even passed on the big budget, all-star movie, *Apollo 13*, so he could do *Seven*, a film with only a $30 million budget.

It was also key to beginning a professional relationship between Pitt and David Fincher that would lead to Pitt's role as Tyler Durden in one of the true iconic films of the Nineties, *Fight Club*. A visionary pop video director who'd made a string of award-winning and mould-busting music videos for artists such as Madonna, The Rolling Stones and Michael Jackson, Fincher had made his directorial debut in 1992 with *Alien 3*. With the first two films regarded as classics, Fincher's job of continuing the success of the franchise was always going to be a monumental undertaking.

But *Alien 3* was savaged by critics and hard-

A SEVEN PACK AND A PALTROW

nosed fans alike – some would say that Fincher wasn't up to the job while others would blame the film's failure on its tortured path to the big screen. But even an absolute dimwit at that time could have seen that Fincher's brooding and dark visual style was something to keep an eye on in the future. It was a shame then that he turned his back on Hollywood after being burnt so badly by the *Alien 3* experience.

It would take a script by 31-year-old Andrew Kevin Walker to bring him back to film directing. And the script was key to everything – Pitt had read it and loved it especially with its (very) downbeat but satisfying ending. While the studio already had another draft in place that featured a much more typical Hollywood happy ending, where the two cops save Mills pregnant girlfriend just in the nick of time, both Pitt and Fincher agreed that they wanted to go with the original script.

Thankfully the studio head (in very un-Hollywood fashion) actually agreed with them and the hunt was on for an actress to play Mills' wife whose head would end up inside that special delivery at the end. Gwyneth Paltrow was Fincher's first choice and she accepted the role. More importantly, Pitt and Paltrow fell for each other straight away. Pitt readily admits that it

A SEVEN PACK AND A PALTROW

was love at first sight for him while Paltrow quipped that it was actually love at second sight for her because she had already fallen for Pitt when at the age of 15, she had seen him in *Thelma And Louise*.

While love blossomed on the set, the shoot, like its subject matter was punishing – Fincher only had Pitt for 55 days because of the star's commitment to appearing in Terry Gilliam's *Twelve Monkeys*. With torrential rain pouring down on the cast and crew throughout the production, Pitt ended up cutting open his forearm right down to the bone during the shooting of the chase scene – which explains the appearance of Pitt's arm in a sling for the final part of the movie and more importantly, according to Pitt, his somewhat gory injury would be the first and only time he'd ever seen the director David Fincher turn 'green'.

There was perhaps another surprising element to the movie that audiences didn't know about at the time – that for all the film's dark content, actually shooting the movie was the one of most fun times Pitt had on a film set and offered a welcome respite after the grueling *Interview With A Vampire* – "Fincher was so damn funny and Morgan Freeman was king, a real gentlemen," he would later recall.

BRAD PITT

A SEVEN PACK AND A PALTROW

Seven opened in September 1995 and subsequently shocked both critics and audiences alike. While many found the lurid post-murder scenes hard to stomach, *Seven* garnered glowing reviews and more importantly, Pitt yet again showed that he had no fear when it came to playing roles which were distinctly un-Hollywood. And his part in *Twelve Monkeys* would prove to show off this quality even further.

But to be frank, the media were far more interested in his relationship with Paltrow at that time. While Pitt and Paltrow enjoyed their first public outing as a couple at the British premiere of *Legends Of The Fall* in April 1995, they weren't so keen on the photos of them that appeared in the press in Europe and online soon afterwards.

Before he headed for the set of *Twelve Monkeys*, Pitt and Paltrow had holidayed on the Caribbean island of St Barts and had spent their time sunbathing in the nude. A plucky French paparazzi subsequently took some snaps of Pitt's bits.

Understandably upset at the subsequent publication of the pictures in the French and then the British press, lawsuits were swiftly dispatched by Pitt as he headed off to Philadelphia to take up his role in *Twelve Monkeys*. The film featured

A SEVEN PACK AND A PALTROW

Bruce Willis as James Cole, a criminal sent back to the past by the authorities to stop a virus that wiped out the human race.

While the shoot itself only required two weeks of Pitt's time, he busied himself with character research for the mental patient and animal activist, Jeffrey Goines, who would play a key role in Willis's quest to discover what triggered the deaths of billions of humans.

"For the role of Jeffrey, we needed somebody magnetic," producer Roven explained about the casting of Pitt. "Someone you were compelled to look at." And Pitt was more than happy to come on board – after all, he was a huge Terry Gilliam fan. "Brad was keen to do the part, one that was so unlike anything he'd tried before," commented Terry Gilliam prophetically in the film's production notes. "He plays a fast-talking, wild, crazed person. I was intrigued by the idea, always like the idea, of casting against type. Brad has taken a leap, a dangerous leap, that's going to amaze people".

It was a leap that would see Pitt taking extreme measure to nail the character of Goines. Perhaps it seems strange for someone who was adverse to all things method for Pitt to book himself in for a two-week course of group therapy

A SEVEN PACK AND A PALTROW

and spend the day on a local psychiatric ward at Temple University hospital in Philadelphia but perhaps it showed that Pitt was finally growing up as a 'serious' actor.

"Brad saw his character as a Charles Manson type, and developed the look of Jeffrey based on some of the people he met at Temple," Gilliam explained. "He developed a hypnotic intense look."

Indeed, Pitt was adamant about losing his pretty boy image – his hair was given a buzz cut from barber hell and his famous baby blue eyes were covered by cross-eyed brown contact lenses. The end result was a viciously funny turn as Pitt showed that he had a natural gift for comedy as well as drama.

The film opened to rave reviews and its success would also mean the reaffirmation of Pitt's almost omnipotent-like star status in the eyes of Hollywood's power mongers – somewhat to the gall of director Terry Gilliam. In an interview with IGN's *FilmForce* in 2000, the director recounted his meeting after the film's successful release with Warner Brothers, the studio that had funded *Twelve Monkeys*. They were congratulating him on the film and Gilliam pointed out to them that it was great that there were intelligent audiences out there who actually wanted to watch a film as

A SEVEN PACK AND A PALTROW

unique as *Twelve Monkeys*.

"They said, 'Nah, nah, nah... There's an easy explanation as to why it was successful...' And I said, 'What's that?' And they said, 'Two words...' And I said, 'What are those two words?' And they said, 'Brad Pitt.' I said, 'Oh... Not even Bruce Willis... Madeline Stowe... The script... The production... Nothing else... Just Brad...' That's the kind of stupidity that reigns in Hollywood. They can reduce something that's complex and intelligent to the name of one actor."

The studio system's faith in the Pitt name would prove vital though to the actor as his next projects would begin to bring his bankability and star status into question. The first box office underperformer was *Sleepers* in 1996. The whole set-up must have seemed ideal. First off, the film's New York location was perfect for Pitt because he was shacked up with Paltrow in her Greenwich Village apartment in the Big Apple.

The film itself boasted a stellar cast including Dustin Hoffman, Robert De Niro, Kevin Bacon and of course Brad Pitt. The plot was a controversial one as well – based on the bestselling book by Lorenzo Carcaterra, it tells the story of four boys who are sent to a detention centre where they

A SEVEN PACK AND A PALTROW

sexually brutalise Kevin Bacon's character, Nokes. Ten years later, and the opportunity opens up for the four, including Pitt to take their revenge on their abuser.

Bringing the book adaptation to the screen was Hollywood director Barry Levinson whose previous hits included *Good Morning Vietnam* and *Rain Man*. To the Hollywood bean counters, *Sleepers* must have seemed like a sure thing at the box office. Alas, it wasn't – while the film cost $44 million to make, it only managed to generate $53 million in the States but Pitt did receive favourable notices for his work and more importantly, it more than signposted Pitt's desire to be perceived as true leading man material.

There was better news when in January 1996, Pitt won a Golden Globe for Best Supporting Actor for his role in *Twelve Monkeys* and he was then Oscar-nominated for Best Supporting Actor. While he was to lose to Kevin Spacey for his role in *The Usual Suspects*, such a nomination only added to Pitt's credibility as a serious actor as a well as bankable name.

It had been a truly remarkable year for Pitt. But he was about to experience his very own 'annus horribilis'.

A SEVEN PACK AND A PALTROW

Brad's best bits no. 5

Seven (1995)

Director: David Fincher
Writer: Andrew Kevin Walker
Co-stars: Morgan Freeman, Gwyneth Paltrow and Kevin Spacey

Pitt's role: as the eager but wet-behind-the-ears copper from the country, Detective David Mills.

Plot: soon-to-retire cop Detective Lt. William Somerset is teamed up with young buck Detective Mills as they investigate a series of horrific murders that are based on the seven deadly sins. Closing in on the serial killer, they are shocked when he turns himself in with devastating consequences.

Choice quote: "Ernest Hemingway once wrote, 'The world is a fine place and worth fighting for.' I agree with the second part." [Somerset's voice-over.]

Awards: nominated for best screenplay by BAFTA and Kevin Spacey picked up a New York Film

A SEVEN PACK AND A PALTROW

Critics Circle award for best supporting actor.

Box office: it gleaned over $100 million at the US box office and made nearly £20 million in the UK alone.

Brad's best bits no. 6

Twelve Monkeys (1995)

Director: Terry Gilliam
Writers: David Webb Peoples and Janet Peoples
Co-stars: Bruce Willis, Madeline Stowe, Christopher Plummer

Pitt's role: As the manic depressive mental patient, Jeffrey Goines.

Plot: when convict James Cole is sent from the future back in time to try and find out how a deadly virus managed to wipe out five billion humans in 1996, he arrives too early – in 1990 to be precise. Placed in a mental asylum, he learns of the Twelve Monkeys, the group believed to be responsible for unleashing the virus on the human race.

BRAD PITT

A SEVEN PACK AND A PALTROW

Choice character quote: "There is no such thing as right and wrong, there's just popular opinion," says Jeffrey Goines

Awards: Pitt's turn as Goines garnered him an Oscar nomination for best supporting actor but he lost out to Kevin Spacey for his performance in *The Usual Suspects*. Pitt could always console himself with a Golden Globe for his performance instead.

Box office: the $30 million movie enjoyed substantial success in the US, drumming up nearly $60 million.

And so he should be smiling... he's come a long way since his role as the sexual-enlightening bad boy J.D in 'Thelma and Louise'. Brad Pitt's varied roles have taken him from fly fishing, to bare knuckle boxing, to blood sucking and, more recently, a Greek warrior.

Brad and actress Jennifer Aniston met in 1988, they married in July 2000. Guests at the wedding included Cameron Diaz, Selma Hayek, Edward Norton and of course, most of the cast of 'Friends'.

Talent and looks, he's a cool character. Just cut-out and keep!

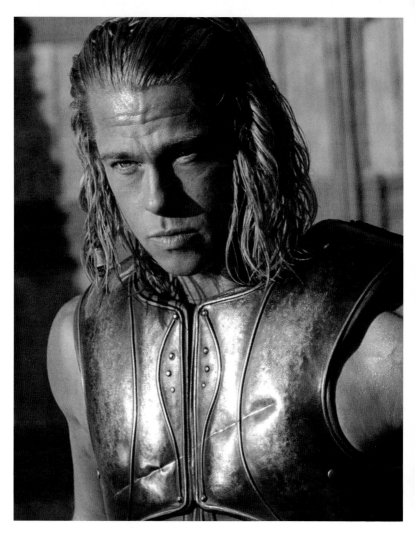

Brad Pitt as Achilles in 'Troy' (2004). The film's locations included London, Mexico and Malta – which played home to one of the world's biggest ever sets with its recreation of Troy. Whilst on set, ironically, Brad actually tore his left Achilles tendon.

8

Brad Pitt meets Charlie Brown

BRAD PITT MEETS CHARLIE BROWN

T*he Devil's Own* had long been something of a labour of love for Brad Pitt. His involvement dated back to 1991 when Pitt signed up to play the role of an IRA gunman who travels to New York to secure Stinger missiles on the black market. Because of Pitt's swelling profile, the film was finally put into pre-production in 1994 and in 1996 Pitt flew to Ireland to begin research on the role.

Perhaps the verbal and physical abuse he received at the hands of two youths who objected to him looking into the window of a Protestant bookshop was a forewarning of the troubles that

BRAD PITT MEETS CHARLIE BROWN

would beset the film. On the face of it, all the key elements were in place: The Oscar nominated director Alan J. Pakula was on board and on Pitt's suggestion, Harrison Ford had been approached. He had accepted the role of cop Tom O'Meara who takes Pitt's character in to his home and then pays the consequences.

The problems started when Pakula wanted to make changes to the script that Pitt had fallen so in love with. Various screenwriters were shepherded in to get to work on the rewrites; the end result made the original script much more politically neutral and also beefed up Ford's role into something decidedly more hero-shaped. And in true Hollywood style, a love interest for Pitt's character was also introduced into the rewrite.

Pitt was unhappy with the new draft and wanted out. He promptly returned after being threatened with a lawsuit by the film's studio Columbia Pictures. Shooting finally began but rumours began to spill out that Pitt and Ford could barely look each other in the eye on set – allegations that were refuted by both actors later..

Unfortunately, matters got even worse once shooting was completed when Pitt stated in an interview in the 3 February issue of *Newsweek* in

BRAD PITT

BRAD PITT MEETS CHARLIE BROWN

1997: "It was the most irresponsible bit of filmmaking – if you can even call it that – that I've ever seen. I couldn't believe it," Pitt said. "This script that I had loved was gone. I guess people just had different visions and you can't argue with that. But then I wanted out and the studio head said, 'All right, we'll let you out. But it'll be $63 million for starters.'"

Pitt would later claim that his comments were taken out of context by *Newsweek* and that he had been simply referring to the pre-production process and not the actual filming itself. Ultimately, Pitt would claim that he was proud of the finished movie but on its release, *The Devil's Own* went on to receive very mixed reviews in the States and the public weren't exactly flocking to see the film either. The budget had swollen up to the $80 million mark and its subsequent takings at the US box office of just over $40 million must have made what was already a difficult experience for Pitt even worse.

Its release in Britain didn't fare much better either with tabloids and Tory MPs piling into the film for its superficial portrayal of The Troubles. Plus Princess Diana's decision to take her two sons to the 15-rated film when Prince

BRAD PITT

BRAD PITT MEETS CHARLIE BROWN

Harry was only 12 at the time also generated more negative publicity.

Perhaps Pitt was hoping that his next film *Seven Years In Tibet* which had already been delayed because of the problematic *The Devil's Own*, would be less controversial but he was to have no such luck. The plight of Tibet and its long-suffering treatment at the hands of the Chinese authorities had already been highlighted by Richard Gere's speech at the 1994 Oscars. Tibet had subsequently become a hot topic especially with the increased interest in Buddhism itself in the Western world. As well as *Seven Years In Tibet*, Martin Scorsese was also about to start shooting *Kundun* with a script by Harrison Ford's wife at the time, Melissa Mathison.

While Gere was initially in the frame to play the famed Austrian mountain climber Heinrich Harrer in *Sevens Years In Tibet*, Pitt was eventually asked because of his stature at the box office. Directed by Frenchman Jean-Jacques Annaud and based on Heinrich Harrer's autobiography, the movie opens on Harrer and fellow climber Peter Aufschnaiter as they head to the Himalayas at the beginning of the Second World War. They are captured by the allies and imprisoned. Making their escape, they end up in Lhasa, the city of Buddhist Tibet where Harrer eventually becomes the tutor of the Dalai Lama.

The subject matter was controversial for many reasons. Both *Seven Years In Tibet* and its rival *Kundun* contained political and cultural issues that angered the Chinese authorities before they even hit the screens.

China's anger included attempts to stop production of the two films and threats to ban the films in their country. Disney (who were Kundun's producers) even hired former US Secretary of State, Henry Kissinger, to act as an advisor on their dealings with China. While such pressure tactics from the Chinese government didn't stop the productions, it did create logistical problems for the shoots themselves. *Seven Years In Tibet*'s shoot had already been delayed because of *The Devil's Own* but once underway, they then fell foul of the Indian government – the film was supposed to be shot in India but the country's government became increasingly nervous about upsetting China and eventually rejected the film.

When shooting finally did get underway in Argentina in September, Pitt's arrival sent the local population into a frenzy. He was surrounded

BRAD PITT MEETS CHARLIE BROWN

by fans at Buenos Aires International Airport – despite the Ministry of the Interior endeavouring to keep things under control. Pitt was then whisked off to Mendoza in the President's private jet and finally reached the movie set that had been set up in the small village of Uspallata. Here again Pitt was besieged by female fans whenever he stepped out of his house – it got so bad that metal walls were constructed round it at the time to keep them out: "I'd never seen anything like it," said B D Wong, Pitt's co-star in the movie. "It's not like with most stars, where people have this mild curiosity. With Brad, it's so visceral, so hormonal. People get all screamy and unmanageable."

But his star popularity with the screaming hordes of fans was nothing compared to his genuine popularity with the people he was actually working with – after all, his generosity would lead to the star helping his housekeeper buy a $40,000 Argentinean home and he'd also cough up $5000 towards a crew member's heart operation plus flying over the wives of 'frustrated' technicians working on the film. He even bought a brand spanking new convertible for his make-up lady. Oh, and to top it all off, there was the small matter of Pitt adopting 14 Argentinean street dogs and finding them loving owners.

While Pitt the populist was busy, Pitt the actor was stretching himself and nailing the Harrer's character's Austrian accent by spending hours with an accent coach – this kind of dedication and commitment to his job made a huge impact on *Seven Years In Tibet*'s director Annaud who saw that Pitt understood how Hollywood can destroy a person – that there are so many victims who may be huge stars but ultimately end up running off into the arms of a therapist because they hate themselves. Why? Precisely because they don't *stretch* themselves and their abilities. It was a flaw that Annaud definitely didn't see in Pitt.

While Pitt's personal development as an actor was never in question, more controversy surfaced about the film itself; namely about the true background of the movie's protagonist, Harrer. What Harrer had failed to mention in his autobiography, and was finally revealed by German magazine *Stern,* was that he had been a member of the SS; a fact made all the more perturbing by the article's accompanying picture which showed Harrer and Hitler standing side by side. While it transpired that Harrer had not been involved in any crimes against humanity, Pitt did concede that he would most likely not have played the part if he'd known about the man's past.

Seven Years In Tibet opened in October 1997 and while Pitt garnered acclaim for his role, it was clear that he was growing increasingly tired of the media's insistent questioning about the film. He hit back with a now famous comment: "Reporters are always asking me what I feel China should do about Tibet. Who cares what I think China should do? I'm a f****** actor. I'm here for entertainment, basically, when you whittle everything away. I'm a grown man who puts on make-up."

Unfortunately, the public just didn't seem that interested in the plight of the Tibetans with the $70 million film only chalking up just over half its budget at the US box office. While professionally Pitt must have been stung by the public's apathy towards the film, he was probably still distracted by his relationship with Gwyneth Paltrow. Or the lack of it.

On 16 June 1997, Pitt's spokeswoman Cindy Guagenti issued a 17-word statement to the media: "Brad Pitt and Gwyneth Paltrow have mutually agreed to end their two-and-a-half year relationship." The press went into overdrive, wondering if this was merely a hoax to distract them from a potential secret wedding between the

BRAD PITT MEETS CHARLIE BROWN

two. But alas, when Paltrow moved out of the couple's New York apartment and moved in with chum, Winona Ryder, such hopes for a wedding photo exclusive were cruelly dashed.

On the face of it, it's not hard to understand why the media were so surprised by the split. After all, only three months before, Paltrow had declared that she had turned down the role of Emma Peel in the film remake *of The Avengers* because she didn't want to be separated from Pitt for so long. He had already agreed to do a film (*Meet Joe Black*) in New York City and Paltrow's film would have taken four months, which was too long to be apart.

A multitude of rumours surfaced over the following weeks – some would claim that Hollywood romances are doomed to fail; that warning would come from Paltrow's dad, TV producer and actor, the late Bruce Paltrow, who ironically was married to an actress himself, Blythe Danner.

The second rumour doing the rounds was that there were irreconcilable differences; that while Pitt was the party-loving man about town, Paltrow was more partial to spending the evening in. Other rumours hinted that Paltrow wasn't too keen on the idea of marriage anyway. However these rumours were counter-spun by claims that Pitt was upset by the idea that if they got married then Paltrow was intending to give up on the acting and settle for the life of housewife and mother to their offspring.

While the rumours and wild speculation would fly thick and fast, in July of 1997, Paltrow would tell *Newsday* that the media's "desperation to uncover a reason [for the breakup] has produced information which is false, unfair and foolish. Not only is Brad Pitt beyond reproach, but he is a man of extreme integrity and goodness."

But she would later reveal in an interview that when they split up, her heart had been broken. And in 2003, she would admit that she had been responsible for the split: "I was the architect of my own misery," Paltrow told the US's ABC *New Primetime* show. "I just made a big mess out of it."

The break up did mean that Pitt wouldn't be starring in their first on-screen coupling together, *Duets* either. Then to add insult to injury, the pictures of a naked Pitt shot by the French paparazzi while he was in that honeymoon phase of his relationship with Paltrow in the West Indies back in 1995 surfaced again in August 1997.

The nude pictures were reprinted and

BRAD PITT MEETS CHARLIE BROWN

published in the August issue of *Playgirl*. Pitt piled in with a lawsuit and after *Playgirl* managed to successfully appeal, Pitt won through in the end and *Playgirl* was forced to withdraw all magazines from distribution.

"I just felt like that really crossed the line," Pitt said at the time. " We were on private property, and this person broke laws to get there. It's just so covert and hideous."

With all the disturbances in his personal life, Pitt forced himself to focus on his work when he began shooting *Meet Joe Black* in August 1997. Never one to shy away from a grim role, Pitt had signed up to play Death in Martin Brest's spin on the 1934 film *Death Takes A Holiday*.

In Brest's version, Death takes over the body of a young man recently killed in a road accident and pays uber successful businessman Bill Parrish a visit to inform him that his time is up. Parrish convinces him to give him more time and then Death goes and falls for Parrish's daughter, Susan.

'When I first sat down with Marty [the director], he was doing his best to describe it," recalled Pitt 1998. "But he said there was no way he could, because it sounded like a Whoopi Goldberg concept movie."

BRAD PITT MEETS CHARLIE BROWN

Pitt was reluctant about the role initially but after reading the script, he came on board because he was drawn to its story of love and loss. On Pitt's suggestion, Anthony Hopkins had also been approached to take on the character of businessman Bill Parrish, and the role of Susan was to be played by up-and-coming young actress Claire Forlani.

Both Hopkins and Forlani, of course, had only good things to say about Pitt while working with him. Hopkins would quip later that he would poke fun at Pitt by asking him if the make-up department could do something about his good looks and hair while Forlani would comment that she was surprised by his humility, humbleness and smarts.

While the shooting on Rhode Island was smooth, there were reports from the set that Pitt seemed distant and there was speculation that on the film's completion, Pitt wasn't happy with his performance. This would be something that Pitt would clarify in an interview in 1998: "I'm a little bit of a perfectionist and I could say that about every one of my films. Always, there's something you get up and I would love a second shot at it. But that is all it ever is."

Perhaps with two film flops though, a broken relationship and an ever intrusive media, it was all

BRAD PITT MEETS CHARLIE BROWN

beginning to catch up with Pitt – 1997 would also see the release of *The Dark Side Of The Sun* that starred a young Brad Pitt which was shot back in 1988. Spending most of the film with his face hidden behind a leather mask, the Yugoslavia-shot film sees Pitt playing Rick, a young man with a horrific skin disease who travels across Europe desperately trying to track down a remedy for his disfiguring ailment; a role that would only pay $1,523 per week for seven weeks' work.

The film was seen as something of an oddity by journalists who were happy to dwell on the gruelling shots of his disfiguring make-up.

All in all, 1997 had been a bad year for the star. As Pitt would quip, it had been his "Charlie Brown year" ("You can have the best intentions, but you're still going to end up with rocks in your Halloween bag.") But perhaps a friend of Brad's summed up the star's 'annus horribilis' best: "If you've broken up with your girlfriend, had a couple of movies bomb and your penis has been on the web, how happy are you going to be?"

But the one thing about Brad Pitt is that he's no quitter. When things go wrong, he's the kind of character that is able to take a step back, reevaluate his life and career – and then step back out with fists flying. Quite literally as it would soon transpire.

9

Punch drunk

BRAD PITT

PUNCH DRUNK

I t's one of those classic mental images that perfectly captures the chasm between 'suits' and 'creatives'. The setting was a preview screening for the top dogs at Fox – the executives and marketing heads were out in force and juiced up about the latest collaboration between *Seven* director David Fincher and star Brad Pitt – the film was *Fight Club*.

As he recalls in his memoirs *What Just Happened?*, the producer Art Linson waited outside the screening room as the preview finished. Executives filed out ashen-faced and bearing fixed smiles – it was amply clear to Linson

PUNCH DRUNK

that the film's content had shocked and stunned them. Muted words of praise were briefly dished out to both Levinson and the director Fincher before the executives hurried back to their offices to ponder if *Fight Club* was going to glean them the kind of career-killing controversy that they really didn't want and seemingly hadn't realised they were going to get.

Perhaps the most telling verbal exchange on that fateful day was when a high-ranking executive at Fox, Tom Sherak, simply asked Linson: "What *is* it?" Linson shot back that it was a great movie; about the disillusionment of young males; about their rage; their emasculation, and that the film was actually funny, damn it.

Sherak's response was that Linson should accompany him the following week to see his psychiatrist and explain to him in what way the film was 'funny.' Perhaps though Fox should have seen *Fight Club*'s controversial content coming from several thousand miles off – after all, the film was based on the startling book by first time author and service mechanic Chuck Palahniuk. On its publication, it was described by *Booklist* critic Thomas Gaughan as: "a dark and disturbing book that dials directly into youthful angst and will likely

PUNCH DRUNK

horrify the parents of teens and 20-somethings."

The book and the subsequent film follows the neutered life of Jack (played by Ed Norton) as an accident investigator for an insurance company. Bored with his product placement of a life, he has taken to attending self-help groups for cancer sufferers to fill his waking hours and help cure him of his insomnia. Disenfranchised Jack eventually hooks up with maverick 'businessman' Tyler Durden on a plane trip and later after a few beers in a bar, the two go outside and proceed to pummel each other in what initially starts out as the ultimate in self-help for the frustrated male of the species.

This simple act leads to the creation of Fight Club where men from all over the city meet and unleash their frustrations with their lives by beating each other up. These events soon turn nationwide and Durden goes a step further by creating Project Mayhem, a movement designed to bring America's corporate and commercial culture to its knees. In a glorious shock ending where Durden's true identity is revealed, the 'two' come to real blows as they face each other off over Project Mayhem and more importantly over the affections of Marla Singer played by

PUNCH DRUNK

Helena Bonham Carter.

Talking about the context of the two lead characters, Pitt would tell *The Calgary Sun* that, "Edward [Norton] and I belong to the first generation raised on TV. We've been sold a lifestyle for as long as we can remember. We have no sense of direction. We've been told that if we have this brand of beer, this style of car and this kind of woman, we have achieved spiritual happiness."

Many taboos were broken in Fight Club, some of which audiences probably didn't even know existed. Nearly every scene contains something to shock even the strongest viewer. Think of Tyler Durden stealing the discarded fat from a liposuction clinic to make soap and Durden demanding to be punched harder by an assailant while laughing hysterically. Then there's the terminal cancer victim hoping to get laid for the last time all washed down with the infamous acid burn scene. It was reported that Pitt showed this scene to his folks to put them off seeing the film in its entirety.

When the movie was released, its detractors were horrified by the violence in the film. Accusations were made that *Fight Club* would

PUNCH DRUNK

encourage men to take to the back alleys to beat seven shades out of each other instead of addressing any of their emasculated hunter/gatherer instincts through a healthy course of group therapy.

It was an allegation that Pitt wasn't convinced by. He commented in an interview with *CNN* in 1999: "The fighting isn't necessarily 'take your aggression out on someone else.' The idea is just get in there, have an experience, take a punch more importantly and see how you come out on the other end – test yourself."

It was obvious though that Pitt was becoming frustrated at all the negative comments being banded about *Fight Club*. He would argue in an interview in 1999 that art must reflect the times in which we live: "It's not the Fifties anymore. Now we've learned that teachers don't always teach, and lawyers aren't necessarily about justice. And doctors aren't always about healing..."

Despite all the controversy, to say that the $63 million film opened to lacklustre box office is something of an understatement. On hindsight, its disappointing performance in the States might in part be blamed on the cack-handed marketing campaign, which merely reduced the complex and layered narrative of the film into 'Brad and Ed beat the daylights out of each other.' Sure, it was the kind of B-movie promotion that Chuck Norris or Steven Seagal would've probably been proud of but hardly the best selling point for one of the darkest, funniest and most challenging films of the Nineties.

The film did fare better overseas and more importantly, once *Fight Club* appeared on DVD and video, it began to fly off the shelves as a refocused marketing campaign – and more importantly, word-of-mouth – took over. The film went on to become one of Fox's best selling DVDs of all time and *Fight Club*, for all the studio execs fears of an impending career post mortem, would end up bringing home a modest $10 million in profit. And also show that yet again that Pitt was more interested in acting than mere 'movie stardom.'

This attitude for taking on challenging parts instead of glamour roles was commented upon by a man who's not known for aiming his tongue anywhere near the derriere of the Hollywood business machine: "One of the true surprises for me during the making of *Fight Club* was Brad Pitt," the film's producer Art Linson would later write in his Hollywood expose *What Just Happened?* in 2002. "He never showed any evidence of an actor who was out there trying to protect his 'Brad Pitt-ness'... I was not expecting Brad to be almost reckless about challenging the boundaries of what others were expecting him to do. His work in *Fight Club* was stellar."

Up next for Pitt would come the equally punch drunk but the altogether more lightweight flick, *Snatch*. It wasn't that the then hot shot director Guy Ritchie was intending for Pitt to appear in his $10 million movie – with a price tag of millions, the idea of casting a star like Brad Pitt was the stuff of pipe dreams. But Pitt had seen Ritchie's feature debut *Lock, Stock And Two Smoking Barrels* and had loved it: "I was so taken by [Lock, Stock], I laughed my hairy ass off," Pitt told *Premiere Magazine* in 2001. Pitt was so drawn to the frenetic energy of the film and the way Ritchie played with the movie's timeline that he knew he wanted to work with the Brit wunderkind.

So Pitt dropped Ritchie a line to ask if there might be a plum role for him in *Snatch*. Enter the Irish Gypsy fighter character of Punch Mickey, just one of the extreme characters that makes up the convoluted story of diamond heists, rigged boxing matches and dodgy 'geezas'. For his role, Pitt had to be 'uglified' – after all, Punch Mickey was supposed to have been involved in bare-

PUNCH DRUNK

knuckle boxing since he was a young boy and those perfectly-chiselled golden boy looks were simply too unrealistic for such a character.

Not only did Pitt have temporary tattoos etched on all over his body that included a Last Supper motif on his back but he also required the obligatory boxer's nose – an effect achieved by adding a false bridge to his nose to make it look thicker. While his stint on *Fight Club* must have helped Pitt's preparation for his character in *Snatch*, he did spend time on a traveller's site near Watford being taught by a gypsy and former boxer Bobby Frankham.

Most important though was nailing Punch Mickey's thick Irish accent: "I had this friend who would do this imitation, and I kind of took from that," Pitt said. "I remember this episode of *Father Ted*... They had one guy on there that only had three lines... [plus] borrowing from Benicio Del Toro in *The Usual Suspects*, we kind of went the incomprehensible route. Then it started to click. But I was sweating, because it didn't happen until the last minute."

In August 2000, the film premiered at the Leicester Square Odeon in London. With 4,000 fans there to see him, Pitt did his star duties by shaking hands with some of them only to be told

PUNCH DRUNK

by police that if he continued, he would be arrested because some of the hormonally-charged mob were starting to get physically crushed in their over-excitement.

But like those throngs of star-struck fans that evening, Pitt himself had been smitten by a Hollywood star – and the lady in question? One Jennifer Aniston, and this time it looked like Pitt was playing for keeps.

Brad's best bits no. 7

Fight Club (1999)

Director: David Fincher
Writer: Jim Uhls
Co-Stars: Edward Norton, Helena Bonham Carter, Meat Loaf.

Pitt's role: as the uber subversive Tyler Durden.

Plot: Jack's stuck in a rut in a dead end job. Even his trips to terminal cancer self help groups can't help him overcome his male middle class malaise. Enter Tyler Durden who turns Jack's world upside down with the creation of Fight Club.

BRAD PITT

PUNCH DRUNK

Choice character quote: "Gentlemen, welcome to Fight Club. The first rule of Fight Club is you do not talk about Fight Club. The second rule of Fight Club is...you do not talk about Fight Club." [Tyler Durden.]

Awards: Helena Bonham Carter picked up an Empire Award for her portrayal of Marla Singer.

Box office: with a $63 million budget, *Fight Club* floundered at the US box office only bringing in $37 million – but the movie went on to become one of Fox's best selling DVDs of all time.

10

Aniston and on and on

BRAD PITT

ANISTON AND ON AND ON

L egend has it that Brad Pitt would meet his future wife Jennifer Aniston not through a chance meeting at an awards ceremony or while hob-nobbing at some swish celebrity-laden party but through a date arranged by their two agents back in 1998. Aniston who the entire world knows as Rachel from *Friends* had been a regular on TV screens from the age of 15 and was no stranger to the world of the celeb – her godfather was Telly Savalas who was best known for his lolly-licking role in *Kojak*.

The relationship sparked off the usual round of headlines as everyone began to immediately

ANISTON AND ON AND ON

wonder when the two would be hitched; who would split with who and when; and when any pregnancy would be announced. Pitt and Aniston, herself no stranger to headline bating after her split with actor Tate Donovan the previous year, would play the relationship close to their chests – they even went out of their way to make sure they weren't photographed together during the early stages of their romance.

Pitt's flair for the romantic would come to the fore again – nine months into their relationship and to celebrate her 30th, Pitt and "my girl" Aniston leapt on a private jet with friends to enjoy an Acapulco weekend beach party. Of course, it was also Valentines Day on that Sunday so in the setting of the 49-room Villa Alejandra owned by one of Mexico's most elite families, Pitt and Aniston danced until the wee hours of the morning. Some would end up referring to this key trip as a "trial honeymoon".

Such an event was one of the many trips that Pitt and Aniston took together over the first year of their relationship that also saw them take in a tour of the Mediterranean and the North African coast.

Unfortunately, there was another woman in Pitt's life around this time – but not a welcome

ANISTON AND ON AND ON

one. In January 1999, 19-year-old Athena Marie Rolando slipped in through an open window at Pitt's home in the Hollywood hills while he was away filming *Fight Club* and spent the day there.

The police were notified by a caretaker that something was amiss at Pitt's homestead and turned up to find her wearing the Hollywood star's clothes – namely his blue hat, black sweat pants and shoes.

Rolando later claimed that she didn't mean for any of it to happen and that she hoped Pitt "has a sense of humour about this." The note discovered in her possession though must have created unease – it was addressed to Pitt and apologised to the star for ruining his and Paltrow's romance, stating that she had put a curse on the relationship.

Rolando would later claim that voices told her to break into Pitt's home and she was subsequently sentenced to 15 days of community service, three year's probation and most unsurprisingly of all, counselling plus a restraining order which forbid her from going within 100 yards of Pitt or his home.

Meanwhile, back on planet Earth, Pitt's parents were introduced to Aniston in August 1999 when they flew out to Hollywood to meet her and they soon fell for her easy charm.

ANISTON AND ON AND ON

Perhaps most importantly was when Pitt approached Aniston's father and asked for his permission to wed his daughter. The young couple had invited John Aniston to join them at a restaurant in LA. The one-time star of US daytime soap *Days Of Our Lives* told *Sunday Magazine* in 2001. "Only Brad showed up, and then he very nervously asked me if he could have permission to marry my daughter."

Permission was given but on one condition: "I said everything would be fine as long as he treated her well... but if he was unfaithful, or made her unhappy in any other way, he would have me to deal with. But Brad said to me, 'Don't worry John, I won't make her unhappy, I promise.'"

While the media had spent thousands of column inches predicting when the couple would marry, it was Pitt's publicist Cindy Guagenti who would deliver the official news. She told reporters in an official statement on 27 July 2000 that Brad Pitt and Jennifer Aniston would be tying the knot... in two days time.

The venue was kept a closely-guarded secret but the ceremony dubbed "the wedding of century" by some in the media would take place at millionaire TV executive Marcy Carsey's beachfront mansion in

ANISTON AND ON AND ON

Malibu. On Saturday, 29 July, the traffic along Malibu's Pacific Coast Highway was closed down and beach access restricted as the big day arrived. Not much could be done though for the mass of boats that had gathered off the coastline.

Two hundred guests mingled in a huge white marquee – the names on the guest included Cameron Diaz, Salma Hayek, Edward Norton, David Arquette and of course most of the cast of *Friends* were just some of the glitterati attending the wedding.

To protect the guests, Pitt and Aniston went out of their way to ensure their privacy. Although they both wanted privacy, they also wanted an outside wedding and did try to get the air space over the mansion cleared. The authorities refused.

Back on ground level, staff were asked to sign a non-disclosure agreement with up to a $100,000 fine if they should suddenly get the urge to go squealing to the papers about the big day's event. Also, the Malibu sheriff was brought in to keep the press away. Whatever concerns Pitt had about the wedding ceremony though were allayed as the ceremony itself got underway: "The press completely backed off," he said afterwards. "It shocked the hell out of me. I was like, 'I love humanity!' It was one of the coolest things I've ever been to."

And you'd hope so as well – after all, reports say that the wedding would end up costing $1 million. An estimated $300,000 went on the catering alone. Other expenses included $100,000 for security and the same amount for the entertainment that included the Gypsy Kings and a 12-year-old Frank Sinatra impersonator, Dakota Horvath. $85,000 was spent on accommodation for the out-of-town guests who were driven from their venue to the ceremony in buses with blacked out windows. Other expenditures included $75,000 on flowers and $20,000 on fireworks.

Only one picture would appear in the press to document that big day – one which had been approved by the couple and featured them as they walked out of the ceremony married. The fee attained for the picture and account of the big day was later donated to charity by the newly weds.

By the end of the day, Mr Brad Pitt and Mrs Jennifer Aniston-Pitt emerged as Hollywood's latest darlings. For a lad who turned up in LA all those years ago with only $325 to his name, it's fair enough to say that things had panned out fairly well for the guy from Missouri.

11

Brad takes a load off

BRAD PITT

BRAD TAKES A LOAD OFF

Fresh from his nuptials, Pitt's next film would see him casting off his cool guy image and go for something decidedly more goofy in *The Mexican*. Playing a hapless gofer for a big time crime syndicate, Pitt's character Jerry Welbach is dispatched to Mexico to find and bring back a fabled pistol. All this is much to the horror of his girlfriend, Samantha Barzel, played by Julia Roberts who is then kidnapped by hitman Leroy (played by *The Sopranos* lead, James Gandolfini) when the hunt for the pistol goes awry.

Pitt was drawn to the part because he wasn't playing an atypical hero blessed with

BRAD TAKES A LOAD OFF

machismo and effortless grace – Jerry's a bit of clutz in other words: "I call this character the anti-McQueen; [there's] nothing cool about him," Pitt said during an interview in 2001. "I just remember reading this funny line about fairness and this character just wanted to be fair and the world to be fair back to *him*."

Of course, the idea of working with Julia Roberts could have hardly dissuaded Pitt from taking the role but some were surprised that it had taken the two this long to team up. Because Pitt and Roberts had already met 15 years previously when they were both struggling actors trying to make it big in Hollywood, why did it take quite so long for an on-screen coupling between the two? "Things have kind of circled the horizon, but it just seemed too obvious for us to jump into," Pitt explained. "It seemed more like retreads of things you'd seen before, so they didn't come to fruition."

What would have also appealed to Pitt and Roberts about their relationship in *The Mexican* was the Hepburn-Tracy banter between their two characters. Or as it transpired in the movie, the constant high-charged verbal outbursts the kidnapped Samantha gives Jerry as she dishes out

BRAD PITT

BRAD TAKES A LOAD OFF

Ricki Lake-like psychobabble to the hapless hero.

Directed by Gore Verbinski who would go on to helm the smash hit *Pirates Of The Caribbean* in 2003, the movie was shot on location in the Mexican village of Real De Catorce. With a modest budget of $35 million and with Pitt taking a reduced fee for the role – "Yeah, my agents are thinking of dropping me because I'm doing more of the same in the next year and a half," he quipped at the time.

The shoot itself would see the cast and crew enjoying tequila after the day's filming wrapped, feasting on finest roasted goat and indulging in big barbecues at the weekend. What was also useful about the location was that it was tough going for the media to get near it as the village is only accessible via tunnels carved out of the surrounding mountains. But if anything, Pitt was starting to show a more patient side towards the ever prying press. Perhaps the fact they had respected his space at his recent wedding had mellowed Pitt: "I know when I go outside, there'll be a van or two and they'll probably follow us [him and Aniston] four out of seven days a week, trying to get something," he would tell reporters in 2001 .

BRAD TAKES A LOAD OFF

While the press may have backed off from Pitt's personal life, *The Mexican* didn't curry much favour with the media on its release in 2001. Perhaps the film's Achilles heel was the lack of romance between Jerry and Samantha to the disappointment of many fans, it seemed strange that for all the hoopla surrounding the teaming of Pitt and Roberts that their two characters only spend a few minutes actually in other's company in the film.

This perceived letdown was dismissed by both Pitt and Roberts – "in spirit, we're together," Pitt would say about their characters at the time – it perhaps though explains the film's limited success at the US box office where it only managed to rack up $66 million. This is no mean feat for a film that cost $35 million to make but with two huge Hollywood stars headlining the movie, one would have expected it to fare far better.

Never mind, Pitt probably thought because he was about go on to another on-screen coupling that would team him up once again with Hollywood legend, Robert Redford in *Spy Game*. Pitt's mentor and director on *A River Runs Through It* back in 1992, the two 'golden boys' were to appear on screen together for the first time

BRAD TAKES A LOAD OFF

as CIA agents in the Tony Scott-directed thriller.

Spy Game tells the story of Nathan Muir played by Redford who is one day short of retirement but discovers that his young protégé Tom Bishop (Pitt) has been arrested in China on charges of espionage. The film shows his struggle with the CIA's top echelon as he tries to get Bishop released, all while flashbacking to Muir's and Bishop's working and personal friendship over the previous years.

Signing up for the movie was something of a no-brainer for Pitt: "The appeal for me in this movie was definitely the opportunity for me to sit across the table from this man [Robert Redford] whose films I've enjoyed all my life," Pitt said in an interview in 2001.

The film was shot over several locations including London, Oxford, Budapest, Berlin, Washington and Morocco which was used as a stand-in after initial plans to shoot in Israel fell through because the sudden escalation of the Israeli-Palestinian conflict in September 2000. The fact that the actors' insurance companies were unhappy with the idea of an Israeli shoot probably figured large as well.

Pitt did meet real-life operatives as part of

BRAD TAKES A LOAD OFF

his research for the role of Tom Bishop and was of course suitably impressed: "[They're] very serious, dedicated, intelligent men," he told *Entertainment Tonight*'s Jann Carl in November, 2001. "[They're] guys who have given up life, relationships and families to do this. It's a much dirtier, uglier, tougher game than we romanticise it as."

The TV interview came two months after the atrocities on 11 September 2001 a fact that obviously concerned Pitt in relation to the espionage-driven *Spy Game*. Two scenes were edited down – in particular one which featured a large explosion – to ensure that noone came out of the cinema offended or upset by such graphic imagery.

When *Spy Game* was released, it garnered solid reviews but the box office takings were something of a disappointment. Not that Pitt had time to contemplate such issues because he went straight from *Spy Game* on to *Ocean's Eleven*, a remake of the 1960 Rat Pack flick. The idea of remaking the film had been kicking round Warner Bros for over a decade, but it was only when screenwriter Ted Griffin turned in his take on the daring heist, where a group of cons rob three casinos in one night, that the project caught the attention of acclaimed director Steven Soderbergh.

BRAD PITT

BRAD TAKES A LOAD OFF

His business partner George Clooney also loved Griffin's take on the original and signed up to play the main character, Danny Ocean, the ex-con who brings the team of crooks together to pull off the robbery of the millennium. It was also Clooney who would approach Pitt about playing his younger best friend, Rusty Ryan.

While Pitt leapt at the chance to play the part, Clooney admits that he did consider stepping aside to let Pitt take on the main role of Danny Ocean as his co-star was a bigger name. But Clooney really believed he was better suited to the Danny Ocean role than Pitt – simply because he thought he looked too old to play the younger Ryan. "I'm only a couple of years older than that f*****, by the way, but Brad looks 25 and I look 45," he quipped.

The appeal for Pitt agreeing to go ahead with the movie was two-fold. The first reason was working with Stephen Soderbergh.

And the second was the idea of featuring in an all-star cast. It hadn't been done in a long time and financially nobody believed it could be done. But it seemed such a great idea that Pitt and the others readily jumped on board.

Indeed, what made *Ocean's Eleven* so unique

BRAD TAKES A LOAD OFF

was that not since the likes of *The Towering Inferno* or *The Great Escape* had the cinema-going public seen such an all-star line-up in one flick. With a cast that would end up including box office heavyweights such as Matt Damon, Julia Roberts, Bill Murray and Andy Garcia, it meant that all the actors had to step away from their normal fees – all were eventually signed up for $35 million in total. Not a bad sum when the likes of Pitt and Roberts were commanding $20 million a film each.

While Pitt might have been used to taking headline roles, he was more than happy to find himself part of an ensemble piece: "It takes the focus off you," Pitt admitted. "You end up focusing on all the other guys, it's such fun. Everyone's holding up their end of the sheet, as with the heist. I guess it's the same with the performances."

The off-set antics were rumoured to be genuinely good-spirited as well. Clooney had already set the tone when he turned up with 11 red bicycles with the names of each gang member stencilled on them. Clooney and Pitt would also go on to become great friends – it was something that Soderbergh would happily capitalise on during Clooney and Pitt's scenes together where he would try and feature them in two shots together as

BRAD TAKES A LOAD OFF

much as possible while trying to avoid individual close-ups.

But while Clooney labeled the golden boy as the coolest man alive, Pitt would end up falling victim to the clown Clooney's infamous pranks where the self-confessed joker would surprise the unsuspecting Pitt by mounting buckets of water over doors. Pitt would tell reporters that it usually took two hours to sort out his hotel room once Clooney had been let loose in it.

Pitt would also enjoy anonymity on *Ocean's Eleven* for the first time in a very long time – and in the casinos of Las Vegas no less. In the film, Pitt's character Ryan disguises himself as a doctor complete with wig and glasses and during the shooting of the doctor scene in the casino, Pitt was able to wander round without anyone actually realising who he was. "Pure freedom" is how Pitt would refer to his impromptu walkabout. He also became enamoured of the wig that was actually the double's wig from the Mike Meyers comedy *Austin Powers*.

While the shoot might have been all fun and japes, when *Ocean's Eleven* hit screens in December 2001, it turned into serious business. The $90 million film raked in a whopping $183

BRAD TAKES A LOAD OFF

million in the US alone. While the film was accused by some of being all style over precious little substance, there was no doubt in the minds of many fans and critics alike that the film was quintessentially, for want of a better word, 'cool'.

More significantly, Pitt fans were starting to see a much more laidback approach to the Hollywood star and his work. While the pressure and stress of having to stay at the top of Hollywood pile seems to be the driving force behind so many of Tinseltown's top glitterati, Pitt had shown, with roles like *Ocean's Eleven* and *The Mexican,* that he wasn't some fussing prima donna worried about his public persona.

This was probably best illustrated by his comic turn in *Friends*. When it was first announced that Pitt was to appear in the hit show alongside his wife Jennifer Aniston, many would speculate that he would take on the chiselled movie star type who sweeps one of the female characters off her feet.

When the show hit the screens in November 2001, his character was something quite different. In 'The One With The Rumor', Pitt played a nerdy school chum of Monica, Will Colbert, who run into each other and end up reminiscing about how fat they used to be. Monica ends up inviting Will for

BRAD PITT

Thanksgiving where he is horrified to see Aniston's character, Rachel, because she used to bully the hell out of him at school. The ensuing verbal (and geeky) cat-and-dog fight is pure *Friends* dynamite and one of Pitt's finest comic turns to date.

As for Pitt and Aniston's real life relationship, well, they were now firmly ensconced in a $13.5 million mansion in Beverly Hills that boasted a tennis courts and a 35-seater cinema. Despite the shoots in Mexico, Budapest, Morocco and Las Vegas, Pitt and Aniston were constantly in touch – either via bill-busting mobile or a quick flight out on the nearest plane.

Career-wise, Pitt had been hoping to work with the Coen Brothers on *To The White Sea*, which had been in pre-production for two years. Due to budget problems though, the film based on the 1993 novel by James Dickey never transpired. 2002 would also be a year of cameo appearances for Pitt. He'd play himself in Steven Soderbergh's *Full Frontal* as he had done in *Being John Malokovich* in 1999. He would also team up with George Clooney again in Clooney's directorial debut *Confessions Of A Dangerous Mind* where he cameoed as Bachelor Brad for no fee.

BRAD PITT

BRAD TAKES A LOAD OFF

For *Sinbad: Legend Of The Seven Seas*, Pitt decided to do away with his good looks altogether when he played the voice of the titular hero in the Dreamworks family flick. It was quite a change for an actor known for appearing in much darker films.

For his work on *Sinbad*, Pitt was given possibly the greatest accolade of his career to date – never mind that Oscar nomination or the Golden Globe win – he was presented with a *Blue Peter* badge. So delighted was he with the award that he dispatched flowers and chocolates to the *Blue Peter* team back in the UK.

While it could be argued that Pitt was taking a more leisurely approach to his work, happy to play along side fellow megastars (or animated characters) rather than headlining in his own movies, 2004 is set to change all that. Brad's all set to come back to the fore as one of Hollywood's greatest stars.

Even if it did mean ruffling some feathers along the way.

12

Brad the builder

BRAD PITT

BRAD THE BUILDER

It wasn't the most auspicious of farewells when Brad Pitt – at the eleventh hour – left the production of the ambitious sci-fi movie, *The Fountain*, a story about a man who hops through time. In fact, he left some crew members furious when he caught a plane out of Australia, the country where the movie was to be shot.

They were upset that while he was of course a-okay, many of the film's workers were left jobless as the film's production floundered. After all, to keep financial backers interested, the production would need to attract another big Hollywood name at very short notice who'd pack

BRAD THE BUILDER

the same kind of punch at the box office as Pitt did to star alongside Cate Blanchett.

While the angry workers would make their feelings amply clear in an open and very frank letter to the *Ain't It Cool News* website, much rumour and speculation would surface as to why Pitt actually went walkies in the first place. Some would say that he didn't like the script; others that he wasn't enamoured of the film's shooting location on Australia's Gold Coast; but perhaps the biggest reason for Pitt pulling out at the eleventh hour could have been summed up in one simple word – Troy.

Maybe it was a career opportunity that was simply too huge to pass up on. Russell Crowe had already enjoyed massive success and acclaim for his role as Maximus in *Gladiator* four years earlier and, at the time of going to press, the Wolfgang Peterson-helmed $150 million epic blockbuster looks set to leave that film in its wake.

Troy is based on Homer's *The Iliad* and has a script by one of the best screenwriters in the business, David Benioff, who brought his novel to the big screen in Spike Lee's *The 25th Hour*. The movie tells the story of two legendary lovers, Paris, Prince of Troy (played by Orlando Bloom)

BRAD THE BUILDER

and Helen, Queen of Sparta (Diane Kruger). The relationship sparks a war when Paris steals Helen away from her husband. Outraged, the King of the Myceneans enrols the self-serving Achilles (played by Brad Pitt) to lead an attack on the gates of Troy.

The film's production has spanned the world including shooting in London, Mexico and Malta – which played home to one of the world's biggest ever sets with its recreation of Troy. The eight-month shoot provided its own fair share of drama – Hurricane Marty piled into second unit work in Mexico while Pitt's legs became the subject of much press speculation when it was reported that a body double's legs had to be used because his were too skinny. And of course, the ultimate in irony was Brad tearing his left Achilles tendon during the shoot.

After *Troy*, Pitt has been busy shooting the thriller *Mr & Mrs Smith*, the story of a bored married couple who both happen to be assassins, and who are then hired to kill each other. It might sound like a Hollywood concept gone too far but it attracted not only Pitt but also Nicole Kidman. Well, for awhile at least – she eventually pulled out due to her busy work schedule but that

BRAD THE BUILDER

woman with the perfect pout, Angelina Jolie, has stepped in to play the role of Mrs Smith. Fans of both the stars though have been far more interested in reading about the reports that Pitt's derriere will be making an appearance in the film.

And that's not all we can expect from Mr Pitt before the year's out. In what is guaranteed to be the most talked-about sequel of 2004, Pitt will be returning to the role of Rusty Ryan in the sequel *Ocean's Twelve*. The film will also see the original cast of the 2001 hit brought together again for three more heists − this time the targets are in Europe with *Ocean's Twelve* swapping the glitz and schmaltz of Las Vegas for the more 'cultured' cities of Rome and Amsterdam. Needless to say, Andy Garcia's character, Terry Benedict, who was ripped off by the gang cons in the first film is also out for some sweet revenge.

The big news is that Catherine Zeta-Jones will also be making an appearance. It may sound like a budget-busting cast but director Steven Soderbergh disagrees: "When we were coming back from doing press in December 2001, I asked everybody if the idea of a sequel appealed and

BRAD THE BUILDER

they were cool," recalled Soderbergh in 2003. "But they had to make a promise: that is, we're gonna be the first sequel in history that costs exactly the same as the first one. And since the scale of the sequel's gonna be even bigger, they're all gonna have to take an even bigger pay cut than last time."

All the above is proof indeed that 2004 will see an extraordinary line-up for Pitt and one which will underline his standing as one of Hollywood's true greats. But it's never that simple with Pitt – he recently made an announcement that yet again has confounded his critics and fans alike. Pitt has decided to become an architect – or to be more precise, serve an informal apprenticeship with Frank Gehry, one of the world's most acclaimed architects who is preparing an £800 million plan to tackle urban blight in a strip of downtown Los Angeles.

The Canadian architect who designed the Guggenheim Museum in Bilbao has brought Pitt on board to advise him on cinema, sports hall and restaurant designs for his LA rebuild plan. To underline just how seriously Pitt is taking this venture, he's already told his agents that he plans to spend over a year learning computer-aided architectural design.

BRAD THE BUILDER

Fans though shouldn't be too surprised at this unexpected turn in Pitt's career path. After all, Pitt's penchant for doing things differently has already been reflected in his many and varied film roles over the past 16 years but more importantly, his love of art and architecture is well known.

Even while waiting for his call at auditions during his early days as a struggling actor, Pitt would be seen drawing and sketching in notebooks. More hints about his future can be picked up on in the various interviews Pitt has given over the years. He's already been busying himself restoring a 1911 Craftsman house up the Hollywood hills and has done architectural computer renderings for a desert-based architectural project. Pitt has revealed that he would like to design a building or something lasting, something hands-on.

While detractors might have the urge to shake their heads and stifle a laugh at such ambitions – after all, they'd say, he's only an actor – perhaps the final analysis of Pitt's future is best left to *Seven/Fight Club* director and close friend David Fincher. In an interview with *USA Today Magazine* in 2003, Fincher surprised

BRAD THE BUILDER

readers when he commented on Pitt's architectural intentions: "The stuff he's doing is truly great.
I think in the end he may be remembered more
for what he'll bring to [architecture] than what
he'll bring to movies."

So it would seem Pitt just can't help it. He
was born to surprise audiences – something that
he's successfully done now for nearly two decades;
always playing against stereotype; always
challenging himself; and always biting at the
hand that may have been feeding him – but was
also forever trying to shove him in a box merely
marked 'pretty boy'.

Indeed, it seems that Pitt is ready to ditch
that title of 'pretty boy' once and for all in the
mind of his critics. He recently stated that in
four years time, his generation of actors and
actresses will be moving out of the way for the
next: "There's a new generation coming up and
we need new voices in the industry," he said. "We
figure that anything we want to do, film-wise, we
have to get out of our systems before kids come
along because they are going to be the priority
and we won't be able to do everything we want to
do then."

Well, it may be a wise and stoical observation

BRAD PITT

BRAD THE BUILDER

– he's also being saying he's ready to settle down and have children with wife Jennifer Aniston – but before one starts thinking that Pitt is bound for his pipe, slippers and architectural drawings, one gets that nagging feeling that Pitt, like Clint Eastwood, Robert Redford and Paul Newman before him, will be up on the silver screen for decades to come whether he's acting or making movies with his film company, Plan B Productions.

After all, it would seem that this so-called 'pretty boy' is all set to continue doing pretty darn good.

13

Filmography

BRAD PITT

A Stoning In Fulham County (1988) – TV movie
Director: Larry Elikman
Screenwriter: Jud Kinberg and Jackson Gillis
Key cast: Ken Olin, Jill Eikenberry, Nicholas
Pryor, Ron Perlman

Cutting Class (1989)
Director: Rospo Pallenberg
Screenwriter: Steve Slavkin
Key cast: Donovan Leitch, Jill Schoelen, Roddy
McDowall, Martin Mull

Happy Together (1989)
Director: Mel Damski
Screenwriter: Craig J. Nevius
Key cast: Patrick Dempsey, Helen Slater, Kevin
Hardesty, Marius Weyers,

The Image (1989) – TV movie
Director: Peter Werner
Screenwriter: Brian Rehak
Key cast: Albert Finney, John Mahoney,
Kathy Baker

BRAD PITT

FILMOGRAPHY

Too Young To Die? (1990) – TV movie
Director: Robert Markowitz
Screenwriter: David Hill and George Rubino
Key cast: Michael Tucker, Juliette Lewis

Across The Tracks (1991)
Director: Sandy Tung
Screenwriter: Sandy Tung
Key cast: David Belafonte, Marisa DeSimone,
Bebe Drake-Massey, Annie Dylan

Thelma And Louise (1991)
Director: Ridley Scott
Screenwriter: Callie Khouri
Key cast: Susan Sarandon, Geena Davis, Harvey
Keitel, Christopher MacDonald

The Favor (1991)
Director: Donald Petrie
Screenwriters: Sara Parriott and Josann
McGibbon
Key cast: Harley Jane Kozak, Elizabeth
McGovern, Bill Pullman

BRAD PITT

FILMOGRAPHY

Johnny Suede (1991)
Director: Tom DiCillo
Screenwriter: Tom DiCillo
Key cast: Richard Boes, Cheryl Costa, Michael
Luciano, Catherine Keener

Cool World (1992)
Director: Ralph Bakshi
Screenwriters: Michael Grais and Mark Victor
Key cast: Gabriel Byrne, Kim Basinger,
William Frankfather, Greg Collins

A River Runs Through It (1992)
Director: Robert Redford
Screenwriter: Richard Friedenberg
Key cast: Craig Sheffer, Tom Skerritt,
Brenda Blethyn, Emily Lloyd

Kalifornia (1993)
Sigurjon Sighvatsson
Director: Dominic Sena
Screenwriter: Tim Metcalfe
Key cast: Juliette Lewis, David Duchovny,
Michelle Forbes

BRAD PITT

FILMOGRAPHY

True Romance (1993)
Director: Tony Scott
Screenwriter: Quentin Tarantino
Key cast: Christian Slater, Patricia Arquette,
Dennis Hopper, Gary Oldman

Legends Of The Fall (1994)
Director: Edward Zwick
Screenwriters: Susan Shilliday and
William D. Wittliff
Key cast: Anthony Hopkins, Aidan Quinn, Julia
Ormond, Henry Thomas

Interview With The Vampire (1994)
Dircctor: Neil Jordan
Screenwriter: Anne Rice
Key cast: Tom Cruise, Kirsten Dunst, Stephen
Rea, Antonio Banderas, Christian Slater

Seven (1995)
Director: David Fincher
Screenwriter: Andrew Kevin Walker
Key cast: Morgan Freeman, Gwyneth Paltrow,
Kevin Spacey

BRAD PITT

Twelve Monkeys (1995)
Director: Terry Gilliam
Screenwriters: David Webb Peoples and
Janet Peoples
Key cast: Bruce Willis, Madeline Stowe,
Christopher Plummer

Sleepers (1996)
Director: Barry Levinson
Screenwriter: Barry Levinson
Key Cast: Kevin Bacon, Billy Crudup, Robert De
Niro, Ron Eldard

Devil's Own (1996)
Director: Alan J. Pakula
Screenwriters: Kevin Jarre, Vincent Patrick and
David Aaron Cohen
Key cast: Harrison Ford, Margaret Colin, Ruben
Blades, Treat Williams

The Dark Side Of The Sun (1997) - Shot in 1988
Director: Bozidar 'Bota' Nikolic
Screenwriters: Andrew Horton and Zeljko
Mijanovic
Key cast: Gus Boyd, Cheryl Pollak, Constantin
Nitchoff, Milena Dravic

BRAD PITT

FILMOGRAPHY

Seven Years In Tibet (1997)
Director: Jean-Jacques Annaud
Screenwriter: Becky Johnston
Key cast: David Thewlis, B.D. Wong, Mako,
Danny Denzongpa

Meet Joe Black (1998)
Director: Martin Brest
Screenwriters: Ron Osborn, Jeff Reno, Kevin
Wade and Bo Goldman
Key cast: Anthony Hopkins, Claire Forlani,
Jake Weber, Marcia Gay Harden

Being John Malkovich (1999)
Director: Spike Jonze
Screenwriter: Charlie Kaufman
Key cast: John Cusack, Cameron Diaz,
Catherine Keener, John Malkovich

Fight Club (1999)
Director: David Fincher
Screenwriter: Jim Uhls
Key cast: Edward Norton, Helena Bonham Carter,
Meat Loaf Aday, Jared Leto

BRAD PITT

FILMOGRAPHY

Snatch (2000)
Director: Guy Ritchie
Screenwriter: Guy Ritchie
Key cast: Jason Statham, Alan Ford, Vinnie
Jones, Ewen Bremner

The Mexican (2001)
Director: Gore Verbinski
Screenwriter: J.H. Wyman
Key cast: Julia Roberts, James Gandolfini,
JK. Simmons, Bob Balaban

Spy Game (2001)
Director: Tony Scott
Screenwriters: Michael Frost Beckner and
David Arata
Key cast: Robert Redford, Catherine McCormack,
Stephen Dillane, Larry Bryggman

Ocean's Eleven (2001)
Director: Steven Soderbergh
Screenwriter: Ted Griffin
Key cast: George Clooney, Julia Roberts,
Casey Affleck, Andy Garcia, Bill Murray

BRAD PITT

FILMOGRAPHY

Full Frontal (2002)
Director: Steven Soderbergh
Screenwriter: Coleman Hough
Key cast: David Duchovny, Nicky Katt,
Catherine Keener

Confessions Of A Dangerous Mind (2002)
Director: George Clooney
Screenwriter: Charlie Kaufman
Key cast: Sam Rockwell, Drew Barrymore,
Michelle Sweeney, George Clooney

Sinbad: Legend Of The Seven Seas (2003)
Directors: Patrick Gilmore and Tim Johnson
Screenwriter: John Logan
Key cast (voice): Catherine Zeta-Jones, Michelle
Pfeiffer, Joseph Fiennes, Dennis Haysbert

Troy (2004)
Rathbun and Colin Wilson
Director: Wolfgang Peterson
Screenwriter: David Benioff
Key cast: Eric Bana, Orlando Bloom,
Diane Kruger, Sean Bean

BIOGRAPHIES

OTHER BOOKS IN THE SERIES

Also available in the series:

Jennifer Aniston

David Beckham

George Clooney

Billy Connolly

Robert De Niro

Michael Douglas

Hugh Grant

Nicole Kidman

Michael Jackson

Jennifer Lopez

Madonna

Shane Richie

Jonny Wilkinson

Robbie Williams

OTHER BOOKS IN THE SERIES

JENNIFER ANISTON

She's been a Friend to countless millions worldwide, and overcame numerous hurdles to rise to the very top of her field. From a shy girl with a dream of being a famous actress, through being reduced to painting scenery for high school plays, appearing in a series of flop TV shows and one rather bad movie, Jennifer Aniston has persevered, finally finding success at the very top of the TV tree.

Bringing the same determination that got her a part on the world's best-loved TV series to her attempts at a film career, she's also worked her way from rom-com cutie up to serious, respected actress and box office draw, intelligently combining indie, cult and comedy movies into a blossoming career which looks set to shoot her to the heights of Hollywood's A-list. She's also found love with one of the world's most desirable men. Is Jennifer Aniston the ultimate Hollywood Renaissance woman? It would seem she's got more than a shot at such a title, as indeed, she seems to have it all, even if things weren't always that way. Learn all about Aniston's rise to fame in this compelling biography.

OTHER BOOKS IN THE SERIES

DAVID BECKHAM

This book covers the amazing life of the boy from East London who has not only become a world class footballer and the captain of England, but also an idol to millions, and probably the most famous man in Britain.

His biography tracks his journey, from the playing fields of Chingford to the Bernabau. It examines how he joined his beloved Manchester United and became part of a golden generation of talent that led to United winning trophies galore.

Beckham's parallel personal life is also examined, as he moved from tongue-tied football-obsessed kid to suitor of a Spice Girl, to one half of Posh & Becks, the most famous celebrity couple in Britain – perhaps the world. His non-footballing activities, his personal indulgences and changing styles have invited criticism, and even abuse, but his football talent has confounded the critics, again and again.

The biography looks at his rise to fame and his relationship with Posh, as well as his decision to leave Manchester for Madrid. Has it affected his relationship with Posh? What will the latest controversy over his sex life mean for celebrity's royal couple? And will he come back to play in England again?

OTHER BOOKS IN THE SERIES

GEORGE CLOONEY

The tale of George Clooney's astonishing career is an epic every bit as riveting as one of his blockbuster movies. It's a story of tenacity and determination, of fame and infamy, a story of succeeding on your own terms regardless of the risks. It's also a story of emergency rooms, batsuits, tidal waves and killer tomatoes, but let's not get ahead of ourselves.

Born into a family that, by Sixties' Kentucky standards, was dripping with show business glamour, George grew up seeing the hard work and heartache that accompanied a life in the media spotlight.

By the time stardom came knocking for George Clooney, it found a level-headed and mature actor ready and willing to embrace the limelight, while still indulging a lifelong love of partying and practical jokes. A staunchly loyal friend and son, a bachelor with a taste for the high life, a vocal activist for the things he believes and a born and bred gentleman; through failed sitcoms and blockbuster disasters, through artistic credibility and box office success, George Clooney has remained all of these things...and much, much more. Prepare to meet Hollywood's most fascinating megastar in this riveting biography.

OTHER BOOKS IN THE SERIES

BILLY CONNOLLY

In a 2003 London Comedy Poll to find Britain's favourite comedian, Billy Connolly came out on top. It's more than just Billy Connolly's all-round comic genius that puts him head and shoulders above the rest. Connolly has also proved himself to be an accomplished actor with dozens of small and big screen roles to his name. In 2003, he could be seen in *The Last Samurai* with Tom Cruise.

Connolly has also cut the mustard in the USA, 'breaking' that market in a way that chart-topping pop groups since The Beatles and the Stones have invariably failed to do, let alone mere stand-up comedians. Of course, like The Beatles and the Stones, Billy Connolly has been to the top of the pop charts too with D.I.V.O.R.C.E. in 1975.

On the way he's experienced heartache of his own with a difficult childhood and a divorce of his own, found the time and energy to bring up five children, been hounded by the press on more than one occasion, and faced up to some considerable inner demons. But Billy Connolly is a survivor. Now in his 60s, he's been in show business for all of 40 years, and 2004 finds him still touring. This exciting biography tells the story an extraordinary entertainer.

OTHER BOOKS IN THE SERIES

ROBERT DE NIRO

Robert De Niro is cinema's greatest chameleon. Snarling one minute, smirking the next, he's straddled Hollywood for a quarter of a century, making his name as a serious character actor, in roles ranging from psychotic taxi drivers to hardened mobsters. The scowls and pent-up violence may have won De Niro early acclaim but, ingeniously, he's now playing them for laughs, poking fun at the tough guy image he so carefully cultivated. Ever the perfectionist, De Niro holds nothing back on screen, but in real life he is a very private man – he thinks of himself as just another guy doing a job. Some job, some guy. There's more to the man than just movies. De Niro helped New York pick itself up after the September 11 terrorist attacks on the Twin Towers by launching the TriBeCa Film Festival and inviting everyone downtown. He runs several top-class restaurants and has dated some of the most beautiful women in the world, least of all supermodel Naomi Campbell. Now in his 60s, showered with awards and a living legend, De Niro's still got his foot on the pedal. There are six, yes six, films coming your way in 2004. In this latest biography, you'll discover all about his latest roles and the life of this extraordinary man.

OTHER BOOKS IN THE SERIES

MICHAEL DOUGLAS

Douglas may have been a shaggy-haired member of a hippy commune in the Sixties but just like all the best laidback, free-loving beatniks, he's gone on to blaze a formidable career, in both acting and producing.

In a career that has spanned nearly 40 years so far, Douglas has produced a multitude of hit movies including the classic *One Flew Over The Cuckoo's Nest* and *The China Syndrome* through to box office smashes such as *Starman* and *Face/Off*.

His acting career has been equally successful – from *Romancing The Stone* to *Wall Street* to *Fatal Attraction*, Douglas's roles have shown that he isn't afraid of putting himself on the line when up there on the big screen.

His relationship with his father; his stay in a top clinic to combat his drinking problem; the breakdown of his first marriage; and his publicised clash with the British media have all compounded to create the image of a man who's transformed himself from being the son of Hollywood legend Kirk Douglas, into Kirk Douglas being the dad of Hollywood legend, Michael Douglas.

OTHER BOOKS IN THE SERIES

HUGH GRANT

He's the Oxford fellow who stumbled into acting, the middle-class son of a carpet salesman who became famous for bumbling around stately homes and posh weddings. The megastar actor who claims he doesn't like acting, but has appeared in over 40 movies and TV shows.

On screen he's romanced a glittering array of Hollywood's hottest actresses, and tackled medical conspiracies and the mafia. Off screen he's hogged the headlines with his high profile girlfriend as well as finding lifelong notoriety after a little Divine intervention in Los Angeles.

Hugh Grant is Britain's biggest movie star, an actor whose talent for comedy has often been misjudged by those who assume he simply plays himself.

From bit parts in Nottingham theatre, through comedy revues at the Edinburgh Fringe, and on to the top of the box office charts, Hugh has remained constant – charming, witty and ever so slightly sarcastic, obsessed with perfection and performance while winking to his audience as if to say: "This is all awfully silly, isn't it?" Don't miss this riveting biography.

OTHER BOOKS IN THE SERIES

NICOLE KIDMAN

On 23 March 2003 Nicole Kidman won the Oscar for Best Actress for her role as Virginia Woolf in *The Hours.* That was the night that marked Nicole Kidman's acceptance into the upper echelons of Hollywood royalty. She had certainly come a long way from the 'girlfriend' roles she played when she first arrived in Hollywood – in films such as *Billy Bathgate* and *Batman Forever* – although even then she managed to inject her 'pretty girl' roles with an edge that made her acting stand out. And she was never merely content to be Mrs Cruise, movie star's wife. Although she stood dutifully behind her then husband in 1993 when he was given his star on the Hollywood Walk of Fame, Nicole got a star of her own 10 years later, in 2003.

Not only does Nicole Kidman have stunning good looks and great pulling power at the box office, she also has artistic credibility. But Nicole has earned the respect of her colleagues, working hard and turning in moving performances from a very early age. Although she dropped out of school at 16, no one doubts the intelligence and passion that are behind the fiery redhead's acting career, which includes television and stage work, as well as films. Find out how Kidman became one of Hollywood's most respected actresses in this compelling biography.

OTHER BOOKS IN THE SERIES

MICHAEL JACKSON

Friday 29 August 1958 was not a special day in Gary, Indiana, and indeed Gary, was far from being a special place. But it was on this day and in this location that the world's greatest entertainer was to be born, Michael Joseph Jackson.

The impact that this boy was destined to have on the world of entertainment could never have been estimated. Here we celebrate Michael Jackson's extraordinary talents, and plot the defining events over his 40-year career. This biography explores the man behind the myth, and gives an understanding of what drives this special entertainer.

In 1993, there was an event that was to rock Jackson's world. His friendship with a 12-year-old boy and the subsequent allegations resulted in a lawsuit, a fall in record sales and a long road to recovery. Two marriages, three children and 10 years later there is a feeling of déjà vu as Jackson again deals with more controversy. Without doubt, 2004 proves to be the most important year in the singer's life. Whatever that future holds for Jackson, his past is secured, there has never been and there will never again be anything quite like Michael Jackson.

OTHER BOOKS IN THE SERIES

JENNIFER LOPEZ

There was no suggestion that the Jennifer Lopez of the early Nineties would become the accomplished actress, singer and icon that she is today. Back then she was a dancer on the popular comedy show *In Living Color* – one of the Fly Girls, the accompaniment, not the main event. In the early days she truly was Jenny from the block; the Bronx native of Puerto Rican descent – another hopeful from the east coast pursuing her dreams in the west.

Today, with two marriages under her belt, three multi-platinum selling albums behind her and an Oscar-winning hunk as one of her ex-boyfriends, she is one of the most talked about celebrities of the day. Jennifer Lopez is one of the most celebrated Hispanic actresses of all time.

Her beauty, body and famous behind, are lusted after by men and envied by women throughout the world. She has proven that she can sing, dance and act. Yet her critics dismiss her as a diva without talent. And the criticisms are not just about her work, some of them are personal. But what is the reality? Who is Jennifer Lopez, where did she come from and how did get to where she is now? This biography aims to separate fact from fiction to reveal the real Jennifer Lopez.

OTHER BOOKS IN THE SERIES

MADONNA

Everyone thought they had Madonna figured out in early 2003. The former Material Girl had become Maternal Girl, giving up on causing controversy to look after her two children and set up home in England with husband Guy Ritchie. The former wild child had settled down and become respectable. The new Madonna would not do anything to shock the establishment anymore, she'd never do something like snogging both Britney Spears and Christina Aguilera at the MTV Video Music Awards... or would she?

Of course she would. Madonna has been constantly reinventing herself since she was a child, and her ability to shock even those who think they know better is both a tribute to her business skills and the reason behind her staying power. Only Madonna could create gossip with two of the current crop of pop princesses in August and then launch a children's book in September. In fact, only Madonna would even try.

In her 20-year career she has not just been a successful pop singer, she is also a movie star, a business woman, a stage actress, an author and a mother. Find out all about this extraordinary modern-day icon in this new compelling biography.

OTHER BOOKS IN THE SERIES

SHANE RICHIE

Few would begrudge the current success of 40-year-old Shane Richie. To get where he is today, Shane has had a rather bumpy roller coaster ride that has seen the hard working son of poor Irish immigrants endure more than his fair share of highs and lows – financially, professionally and personally.

In the space of four decades he has amused audiences at school plays, realised his childhood dream of becoming a Pontins holiday camp entertainer, experienced homelessness, beat his battle with drink, became a millionaire then lost the lot. He's worked hard and played hard.

When the producers of *EastEnders* auditioned Shane for a role in the top TV soap, they decided not to give him the part, but to create a new character especially for him. That character was Alfie Moon, manager of the Queen Vic pub, and very quickly Shane's TV alter ego has become one of the most popular soap characters in Britain. This biography is the story of a boy who had big dreams and never gave up on turning those dreams into reality.

OTHER BOOKS IN THE SERIES

JONNY WILKINSON

"There's 35 seconds to go, this is the one. It's coming back for Jonny Wilkinson. He drops for World Cup glory. It's over! He's done it! Jonny Wilkinson is England's Hero yet again..."

That memorable winning drop kick united the nation, and lead to the start of unprecedented victory celebrations throughout the land. In the split seconds it took for the ball to leave his boot and slip through the posts, Wilkinson's life was to change forever. It wasn't until three days later, when the squad flew back to Heathrow and were met with a rapturous reception, that the enormity of their win, began to sink in.

Like most overnight success stories, Wilkinson's journey has been a long and dedicated one. He spent 16 years 'in rehearsal' before achieving his finest performance, in front of a global audience of 22 million, on that rainy evening in Telstra Stadium, Sydney.

But how did this modest self-effacing 24-year-old become England's new number one son? This biography follows Jonny's journey to international stardom. Find out how he caught the rugby bug, what and who his earliest influences were and what the future holds for our latest English sporting hero.

OTHER BOOKS IN THE SERIES

ROBBIE WILLIAMS

Professionally, things can't get much better for Robbie Williams. In 2002 he signed the largest record deal in UK history when he re-signed with EMI. The following year he performed to over 1.5 million fans on his European tour, breaking all attendance records at Knebworth with three consecutive sell-out gigs.

Since going solo Robbie Williams has achieved five number one hit singles, five number one hit albums; 10 Brits and three Ivor Novello awards. When he left the highly successful boy band Take That in 1995 his future seemed far from rosy. He got off to a shaky start. His nemesis, Gary Barlow, had already recorded two number one singles and the press had virtually written Williams off. But then in December 1997, he released his Christmas single, *Angels.*

Angels re-launched his career – it remained in the Top 10 for 11 weeks. Since then Robbie has gone from strength to strength, both as a singer and a natural showman. His live videos are a testament to his performing talent and his promotional videos are works of art.

This biography tells of Williams' journey to the top – stopping off on the way to take a look at his songs, his videos, his shows, his relationships, his rows, his record deals and his demons.